The Paradoxes o

Éliphas Lévi

THE PARADOXES

OF

THE HIGHEST SCIENCE

IN WHICH THE MOST ADVANCED
TRUTHS OF OCCULTISM
ARE FOR THE FIRST TIME REVEALED
(IN ORDER TO RECONCILE
THE FUTURE DEVELOPMENTS OF
SCIENCE AND PHILOSOPHY
WITH THE ETERNAL RELIGION)

Éliphas Lévi

With Footnotes by
A Master of the Wisdom

Introduction by R. A. Gilbert

Ibis Press
An Imprint of Nicolas-Hays, Inc.
Berwick, Maine

First published in 2004 by
Ibis Press
An Imprint of Nicolas-Hays, Inc.
P. O. Box 1126
Berwick, ME 03901-1126
www.nicolashays.com

Distributed to the trade by
Red Wheel/Weiser, LLC
P. O. Box 612
York Beach, ME 03910-0612
www.redwheelweiser.com

Library of Congress Cataloging-in-Publication Data is
available
TP

Cover and text design by Phillip Augusta.

Typeset in Monotype Old Style

Printed in Canada

10	09	08	07	06	05	04
7	6	5	4	3	2	1

The paper used in this publication meets the minimum
requirements of the American National Standard for
Information Sciences—Permanence of Paper for Printed
Library Materials Z39.48–1992 (R1997).

CONTENTS

Preface..*vi*
Foreword..*xi*
Introduction by R. A. Gilbert................................*xii*
Errata..

PARADOX

I. Religion is magic, sanctioned by authority............1
II. Liberty is obedience to the Law.........................16
III. Love is the realisation of the impossible.............32
IV. Knowledge is the ignorance or negation of Evil..41
V. Reason is God...57
VI. The Imagination realises what it invents............74
VII. The Will accomplishes everything which it does
  not desire..88

Synthetic Recapitulation—Magic—Magism.................*98*
The Unalterable Principles......................................*135*
The Great Secret..*159*

PREFACE
To the 1922 Second Edition

MANY paths lead to the mountain-top, and many and diverse are the rifts in the Veil, through which glimpses may be obtained of the secret things of the Universe.

The Abbé Louis Constant, better known by his *nom de plume* of ÉLIPHAS LÉVI, was doubtless a seer; but, though his studies were by no means confined to this, he *saw* only through the medium of the kabala, the perfect sense of which is, now-a-days, hidden from all *mere* kabalists, and his visions were consequently always imperfect and often much distorted and confused.

Moreover, he was for a considerable portion of his career a Roman Catholic priest, and as such had to keep terms, to a certain extent, with his church, and even later, when he was unfrocked, he hesitated to shock the prejudices of the public, and never succeeded in even wholly freeing *himself* from the bias of his early clerical training. Consequently he not only erred at times in good faith, not only constantly wrote ambiguously to avoid a direct collision with his ecclesiastical chiefs or current creeds, but he not unfrequently put forward Dogmas, which, taken in their obvious straightforward meanings, he certainly did not *believe*—nay, I may say, certainly knew to be false. It is quite true that, in many of these latter cases, an undercurrent of irony may be discerned by those who know the truth, and that in all the enlightened can sufficiently read between the lines to avoid misconceptions. But these defects, the ineradicable bias of his early training, the very narrow standpoint from which he regarded occultism, and the limitations to free expression imposed on him by his position and temperament, seriously detract from the value of all Éliphas Lévi's writings.

Still, he was an eloquent and learned man, and sufficiently advanced in occultism to render all he wrote on this subject interesting and more or less valuable to earnest students of the Mysteries; and I have, therefore, thought that fellow-searchers for the Hidden Truth would be well pleased to obtain access to some important and hitherto unpublished writings of this great kabalist.

Hence this translation, which, although absolutely without pretensions to literary merit, yet does, I hope and believe, everywhere fully and faithfully reproduce the *obvious* meanings of the author, leaving, in all cases, where this is so in the original, an inner meaning discernible by those who KNOW. If in many places the language appears constrained and awkward, this has arisen from the necessity of preserving intact the exoteric and esoteric meanings, which our author so loved to combine in his epigrammatic sentences.

An eminent occultist, E. O., had added a few notes to the MSS. before it reached my hands, and these, which I have reproduced (though some of them will seem scarcely *relevant* to the uninitiated), merit the most careful attention. I too have here and there ventured a few remarks, which must be taken for what they are worth. I do not always agree with E. O., and, though perfectly aware that my opinion is as nothing when opposed to his, I did not think it honest to reproduce remarks, which I could not concur in, without recording my dissent.

For the rest, any reader who, interested in these Paradoxes, yet feels uncertain at their conclusion that he has fully grasped the author's meaning and desires to know more of this, may with advantage study Éliphas Lévi's other works, viz.—

DOGME ET RITUEL DE LA HAUTE MAGIE.
HISTOIRE DE LA MAGIE.
LA CLEF DES GRANDS MYSTÈRES.
LA SCIENCE DES ÉSPRITS.
LE SORCIER DE MEUDON.
FABLES ET SYMBOLES.

Each one of these amongst, it must be admitted, a mass of irrelevant and I had almost said *trashy* matter, redeemed only by a grace of style necessarily lost in any translation, throws some light upon each one of the others; and no one with any natural capacity for occultism can study these carefully, along with what is now published, without clearly apprehending our author's views. These, however limited and imperfect, were yet, to a great extent and so far as they went, correct, and were moreover, if nothing else, far in advance of most existing and accepted *exoteric* cosmogonies, theogonies and religions.

One word more: Occultism has its Physics and Metaphysics, its practical and theoretical sides. Éliphas Lévi was a theorist and, if we may judge from the nonsense given in great detail in his RITUEL DE LA HAUTE MAGIE, profoundly ignorant of its practice. Of the Physics of Occultism nothing of any great value can be gathered by the uninitiated from his pages, though reproducing, apparently without by any means fully comprehending them, phrases and ideas from the older Hermetic works; secrets, even pertaining to *this* branch, lie buried, like mutilated torsos, in his writings. But where the Metaphysics of Occultism are concerned his works are often encrusted with real jewels that would shine out far more clearly into the soul of the uninitiated but for his persistent habit of laying on everywhere coats of Roman

Catholic and orthodox whitewash, partly in his earlier days to avert the antagonism of the church, partly to avoid shocking the religious prejudices of his readers, and partly, I suspect, because to the last some flavour of those prejudices clung even to his own mind.

To those then who desire to acquire proficiency in Practical Occultism, who crave long life, gifts and powers, and a knowledge of the hidden things and laws of the universe, a study of Éliphas Lévi's books would be almost time wasted. Let them seek elsewhere for what they want, and *if they seek in earnest they will surely find it.*

But by those who, careless of such things, desire only to grapple with and assimilate the highest and ultimate TRUTHS of Occultism more may perhaps be gleaned from his pages by thoughtful study, than from those of any writer, past or present, *whose works are readily accessible to the world.*

To such seekers I say, study Éliphas Lévi's works as a whole and ponder over them. Doubtless they are encumbered by a mass of what, but for the elegance of the diction, would deserve to be set down as twaddle. Doubtless our Abbé was a true Frenchman, often aiming more at felicity of expression and neatness of antithesis than at the simple truth, and ever ready to jump from the sublimest spiritual truth to some cynical mundane jest by no means always in the best possible taste. Doubtless too he perpetually wastes time (for most modern readers) in slaying over again the already defunct bugbears, bogies and monsters of the Roman Catholic Church.

But none the less had he much real occult learning, and this, though in a purposely bewildering, inconsecutive and incoherent form, he put piecemeal on record in his various works.

Truly, though wrapped by his eloquence in cloth of
gold, not an inviting heap! Yet, despite the mass of shells
and sand and ancient fishy odours, the pearls are there
for those who truly seek. A hint in one work, a banter-
ing falsehood in one passage, will explain veiled truths
in others; to those who strive hard to grasp them his real
meanings will become clear; and though the labour be
considerable and the results, even when obtained, imperfect and requiring to be supplemented elsewhere, the
trouble will not have been wasted; and those who have
advanced thus far will assuredly find unexpected help in
completing their task.

THE TRANSLATOR

FOREWORD
To the 1922 Second Edition

THERE appear, in the early volumes of *The Theosophist*, several fragments called "Unpublished Writings of Éliphas Lévi." "Éliphas Lévi" was the French Abbé Louis Constant, a priest who left the Roman Catholic Church to devote himself to Kabbalistic Mysticism. One of these "unpublished writings"—which however was not printed in *The Theosophist*, but separately as a pamphlet, in the series "Theosophical Miscellanies"—was commented upon in footnotes by "E. O.", "Eminent Occultist." Éliphas Lévi's essay, together with E. O.'s footnotes, was then published, and the present publication is a reprint of this "Theosophical Miscellany" printed in Calcutta in 1883.

There would be no point in reprinting this old "propaganda literature" of the early days of the Theosophical Society, but for the fact that "Eminent Occultist" is the Master of the Wisdom now well known among Theosophists under the initials "K. H." It is in a footnote of the Master, in 1883, that first appears in Theosophical literature the assertion that Jesus Christ lived a century B. C. Surely nothing could be more beautiful about woman's rôle in life than what He says in the last of His footnotes.

Reading these notes of the Master has inspired me and given me an insight into His mind. I have urged their republication, hoping that others may receive from them what I have received.

C. J.

INTRODUCTION
To the 2003 Edition

AT the time of Éliphas Lévi's death in 1875, many of his later writings remained unpublished and the manuscripts were subsequently scattered among his disciples in France, England, and elsewhere in Europe. Most of them eventually appeared in print, either in the original French or as translations. The first to be published was *The Paradoxes of the Highest Science*, although as a translation, without any fanfare and far removed from Paris and the world of Western hermeticism in which it was created. It formed the second of a series of "Theosophical Miscellanies," issued at Calcutta in 1883 under the aegis of the Theosophical Society, and presented as "Unpublished Writings of Éliphas Lévi." Both the "Student of Occultism" who translated the text, and the "Eminent Occultist" who provided additional comments, were unsympathetic to the text and plainly ignorant of the author's life (e.g. both of them state, wrongly, that Lévi was an unfrocked priest). For the anonymous translator, Lévi's principal works all contain "a mass of irrelevant and . . . almost . . . *trashy* matter" and he damns Lévi with faint praise. His sole reason for issuing the translation is the thought that students of occultism "would be well pleased to obtain access to some important and hitherto unpublished writings of this great kabalist." Why, then, was the book issued at all?

The Paradoxes comprises a collection of loosely linked aphorisms, principles, and paradoxes related to Lévi's theories of occultism. They are replete with irony and verbal witticisms—the force of which are inevitably lost in translation—and they represent their author's return, late in life, to the radicalism of his youth. But Lévi had synthesized his radical religious ideas with the esoteric doctrines that he developed in his maturity, and attempted to reconcile religion with "science" (in an abstract philosophical sense of the word). Such an approach should have appealed to theosophists, given the motto of the Theosophical Society—"There is no religion higher than Truth"—and that *Isis Unveiled* is concerned with the "Mysteries of Ancient and Modern Science and Theology." In addition, H. P. Blavatsky frequently expressed her admiration for Éliphas Lévi's magical and kabbalistic writings and quoted from them approvingly.

One aspect of Lévi's life and writing, however, she could not stomach: his continuing commitment to the Roman Catholic Church. Despite having renounced his clerical vocation, Lévi never left the Church and remained committed to the Christian faith. Unlike Mme. Blavatsky, his occultism and his religion were both thoroughly Western. It is thus probable that *The Paradoxes* was published because it gave her an opportunity to trumpet the superiority of Eastern over Western esotericism, by way of belittling the work of the greatest Western magician and kabbalist of his day and overlaying it with glosses drawn from her own "Neo-Buddhism" (as her peculiar philosophical system was named by contemporary critics). And it was undoubtedly she who did this, for whereas the "Student Occultism" remains anonymous, "Eminent Occultist" could have been none other than H. P. Blavatsky herself.

She was not only an admirer of Lévi's work, but also encouraged the publication of his manuscripts: there are frequent contributions of his previously unpublished letters and essays in *The Theosophist* from 1881 onwards and xiv

in *Lucifer* in later years. That she would have annotated the manuscript of *The Paradoxes* is thus highly likely, but this is not all. Her style and her prejudices are both easy to identify, and all the hallmarks are present in the comments of "Eminent Occultist." Her violent hostility to Christianity—raised to a venomous degree when she touches on Catholicism—appears frequently, as does her fondness for specious reasoning on the basis of misquoted authorities, and her almost pathological antipathy to the Jesuits.

Whether the translator indentified her or not is unclear, but what is certain is that Curupumullage Jinarajadasa, who arranged for *The Paradoxes* to be reprinted in 1922, did not do so. Although he gives no reason for his conviction and simply makes a dogmatic statement about the identity, Jinarajadasa had convinced himself that "Eminent Occultist" was the "Master of Wisdom," the Mahatma known as Koot Hoomi. If this was the case, then the notes would take on the significance of Holy Writ, and it was for this reason alone that Jinarajadasa wished them to be re-issued. He saw no other point in "reprinting this old 'propaganda literature'" than the benefit that the words of the Master would bestow upon the reader.

Such a bizarre critical viewpoint would be untenable today, when the Mahatmas have returned to the phantom world from which Mme. Blavatsky conjured them up, but it was Jinarajadasa's enthusiasm alone that rescued *The Paradoxes* from oblivion. For so doing he deserves thanks, because there are sound reasons for arguing that the book was well worth the rescue for its own sake. They all surround the person of Éliphas Lévi himself.

The real justification for re-issuing *The Paradoxes* is

Lévi's significance in the history of Western esoteric thought. More than any other writer of the 19th century, he set the course of magical theory and practice for future generations of Western occultists. His "magic," as presented in *Dogme et Rituel de la Haute Magie* (1856), is not the theurgy of Renaissance hermeticists, but an enticing blend of traditional magical practice with a highly original theoretical underpinning, ideally suited to the Romantic era. This extraordinary magical structure was completed with a dramatic and exotic—but utterly unreliable—history (*Histoire de la Magie*, 1860), and a detailed explanation of the theory of magic and of occultism in general (*La Clef des Grands Mystères*, 1861).

Lévi's originality, his genius perhaps, lies in his synthesis of the disparate elements of the Western hermetic tradition. He drew on contemporary theories about Animal Magnetism and Spiritualism and argued that there is an all-pervading, fuidic ether underlying the material world. He named this interior, non-empirical realm "The Astral Light," and peopled it with elementals and other orders of spiritual beings. And it is through the Astral Light that the signs and wonders of magic are mediated.

The secrets of this inner world had been known to the ancient Egyptians, but were lost to European civilization—until Éliphas Lévi came to reveal them again. They lie hidden, he claimed, in the Hebrew Kabbalah and in the symbols of the tarot trumps. This was not an original claim; Court de Gebelin had set the Egyptian hare running with his interpretation of the tarot in the final volume of *Le Monde Primitif* (1784), while the Hebrew language had been dissected, and its esoteric significanee laid bare, by Fabre d'Olivet in *La langue hebraïque restituée* (1816). But Lévi made an extraordinary leap of imagination and related each tarot trump to a letter of the Hebrew alphabet. This set of correspondences has neither a linguistic nor a historical basis, but it has become deeply embedded in tarot symbolism, and it is now an integral part of Western esoteric theory.

The reverence accorded to Lévi's theories, and the enduring popularity of his major works, is largely due to the engaging and racy style of his writing. He was also a talented artist and illustrated his books with symbolic diagrams, tarot designs and dramatic images, such as the Goat of Mendes, which have acquired iconic status. So well did this carefully constructed combination of words and images fit the mood of both would-be occultists and true hermeticists, that Éliphas Lévi may justly be said to have given birth to modern occultism.

But what of the magus himself? Alphonse Louis Constant, for that was his real name, was born on February 8, 1810, into a poor but devout Catholic family, in the heart of Paris. He was a solitary dreamer, displaying a precocious religiosity that suggested a vocation for the priesthood. His studies to this end began in 1825, but by the time he was ordained as a Deacon, in 1835, he had begun to write poetry—perhaps as an escape from his disenchantment with the Church hierarchy—and had realized that he was unable to commit himself to the celibate life of a priest. Despite this, he did not relinquish his faith.

By 1838 Constant had tried his hand at both teaching and acting, and was employing his literary and artistic skills in the cause of the radical political circles in which he moved. This brought him into trouble with the authorities: in 1841 he was gaoled for eight months for writing an inflammatory book, *La Bible de la Liberté*. The Church proved forgiving, however, and, after he was employed to produce a number of religious paintings, Constant was sent to Normandy to assist the Bishop of Evreux. In 1844 his resumed clerical career came to an end when he published a devotional, but doctrinally suspect, book *La Mère de Dieu*.

Returning to Paris and his radical friends, Constant took up old friendships, including that with Eugénie C.,[1] the headmistress of a girl's school. Eventually they became lovers and a son was born on September 29, 1846, but it was not a happy event. Three months earlier, on July 13, Constant had married Noémi Cadiot, a seventeen-year-old pupil of Eugénie. After such perfidy Constant was denied any access to his son. Perhaps he took consolation in his and Noémi's daughter, Marie, who was born in September of 1847.

Initially the marriage was happy; Mme. Constant fully supported her husband's career as a writer of polemics, painter of religious pictures, and, surprisingly, editor of the *Dictionnaire de littérature chrétienne* (1851) for the Migne library. She also took up writing and painting herself, but this led to a liaison with the editor of a "progressive" journal, and at the end of 1853 Noémi Constant left her husband and obtained a legal separation. They were finally divorced in 1865.

Perhaps aware of his wife's infidelity, Constant had already, in 1852, sought solace in occultism and had become a disciple of Joseph-Marie Hoëne Wronski (1778-1853), a Polish savant who was variously a math-

---

[1] In his biography, *Éliphas Lévi, Rénovateur de l'Occultisme en France* (1926), Paul Chacornac omits Eugénie's surname "par un sentiment respecteux" ["out of respect"].

ematician, mystic, prophet, and kabbalist. Wronski was a major influence upon the Abbé Constant, and the decisive factor in his becoming a writer on magic and the kabbalah. Soon after Wronski's death, Constant marked the change in his life's direction by writing *Dogme et Rituel de la Haute Magie.* When the book was completed he marked his rebirth as a magician by placing his new name (a Hebraised version of his Christian names) on the title-page: Éliphas Lévi.

Even before the book was published, in 1856, Éliphas Lévi was gaining a reputation as a magician. In *Dogme et Rituel,* he recounts a visit to London in 1854, when he evoked Apollonius of Tyana to visible appearance for the benefit of Sir Edward Bulwer-Lytton. Whether or not the story is true, it was believed to be so, and both French and English occultists (including both Hockley and Mackenzie) began to make pilgrimages to Paris to visit the now-famous magus. Lévi repaid their homage with a second visit to London in 1861, when he called again upon Bulwer-Lytton and also met the exiled French prophet, Eugène Vintras.

For the next fourteen years, until his death on May 31, 1875, Lévi continued to produce further works on magic, the kabbalah, symbolism, and the nature of the spirit world. As they appeared, so they brought him new disciples, notably the hand-reader Adolphe Desbarolles, Jean-Baptiste Pitois, who is better known as "Paul Christian," author of *Histoire de la Magie* (1870), and the Baron Nicholas-Joseph Spedalieri, whose fascinating and highly important correspondence with Lévi was published in *Lucifer* in 1894 and 1895. And as a teacher of the Western esoteric tradition he gained a respect far beyond anything that had been accorded to the Abbé Constant.

During his final years, Lévi wrote almost ceaselessly, although none of his later work was published during his lifetime, returning frequently to the fervor of his earlier radical views. In some of his works, he attempted to synthesize political radicalism with the kabbalah and a spiritualized Catholicism tinged with apocalyptic prophecy, but the resulting texts (e.g. *Le Livre des Splendeurs*) are often difficult to interpret. Others are more clearly related to the major themes of the Western hermetic tradition, but only *The Paradoxes of the Highest Science* revisits his radical, Catholic youth.

It was not well-received in translation. The text had no appeal for Aleister Crowley (who believed himself to be a reincarnation of Lévi, despite their diametrically opposing viewpoints), and A. E. Waite, who first brought Lévi to a wide readership in the English-speaking world, reduced *The Paradoxes* to occasional citations in his Éliphas Lévi anthology, *The Mysteries of Magic* (2nd ed. 1897) Even Dr. Westcott, who brought Lévi into his pantheon of Golden Dawn saints, and who utilized some of his Maxims in the English translation of *The Magical Ritual of the Sanctum Regnum* (1896) made no reference to it.

The Paradoxes does not deserve such neglect. It is true that it tacks the soaring flights of fancy that characterize Éliphas Lévi's magical works, but it gives us a more accurate glimpse into the mind of its author: the mind, moreover, of a man who—unwittingly and unwillingly, but far more certainly than the theosophical Masters—became the first occult Messiah.

R.A. Gilbert

ERRATA

Please note the following typographical errors in the 1922 Adyar edition of *The Paradoxes of the Highest Science*:

p. 129 "Paschalis, Martines and St. Martin" should be "Martines de Pasqually [or "Paschalis"] and St. Martin"

p. 150 "St. Vincent de Lerius" should read "St. Vincent de Lerins"

p. 161 "Bernadette Soubirons" should read "Bernadette Soubirous"

p. 162 "Berbignier" should read "Berbiguier"

THE PARADOXES OF THE HIGHEST SCIENCE

Paradox I.—RELIGION IS MAGIC SANCTIONED BY AUTHORITY

MAGIC is the divinity of man conquered by science in union with faith; the true Magi are Men-Gods, in virtue of their intimate union with the divine principle. They are without fear and without desires; they are dominated by no falsehood; they share no error; they love without illusion and suffer without impatience, for they leave all to happen as it may, and repose in the quietude of the eternal thought. They lean upon religion, but religion does not weigh on them; religion is the Sphynx which *obeys*, but never devours *them*. *They* know what religion is, and they feel that it is necessary and eternal.

For debased souls religion is a yoke imposed, through self-interest, by the poltrooneries of fear and the follies of hope. For exalted souls religion is a force, springing from an intensified reliance in the love of humanity.

Religion is the collective poesy of great souls. Her fictions are more true than Truth itself; vaster

than Infinity ; more lasting than Eternity ; in other
words, they are essentially paradoxical.

They are the dream of the Infinite in the Unknown,
of the Possible in the Impossible, of the Definite in
the Indefinable, of Progress in the Immutable, of
Absolute Being in the Non-existent.

They are the ultimate rationale of the Absurdity,
which affirms itself, to deny doubt ; they are the
science of foolishness, the embrace of Folly and
Knowledge. They are the cries of the eagle mount-
ing above the clouds, the roar of the lion of the
Apocalypse, that takes to itself wings and flies away ;
the bellowing of the bull beneath the sacrificial knife,
and the never ending moan of mankind before the
portals of the tomb.

*For man, God is, and can only be, the ideal of
man.* In himself, he is the unknown, but in his
revelation, at once divine and human, he is paradoxical man, the substantial without substance, the
personal without definition, the immutable which
transforms itself but has no form, the omnipotent ever
struggling with the weakness of man, the serenity
which thunders, the mercy which damns, the infinite
goodness which tortures, the eternity which perishes ;
an infinite contradiction ; the abyss of the human
heart, serving as a world for an insatiable and terrifying idol ; the cruelty of Nero, the policy of Tiberius
drinking the blood of Jesus Christ,[1] a pope emperor,
or an emperor antipope, the king of kings, the pontiff

---

[1] The Western Ideal of Good.—E. O.

of pontiffs, the executioner of executioners, the physician of physicians, the liberator of the free, the inflexible master of slaves.

God is everywhere the ideal of those who ignorantly adore him ; ferocious amongst savages, instinct with human passions amidst the Greeks, an Oriental despot for the Jews, jealous and merciless for the Ultramontanes as a celibate priest. One and all create a personage whom they endow in an infinite degree with their own characteristics and their own defects. [1]

---

[1] In a Review of Wilson's " Chapters on Evolution " in *Knowledge* for February 23rd, 1883, the following passage occurs showing how Western science is slowly drifting into the position occupied for thousands of years by the Occultists :—

" Quite early the tendency of the Theory of Evolution was seen to be towards the widest possible generality. It was recognised that man could not possibly be excluded from the Law of Evolution. Those who had believed in his nobler origin from the dust of the earth were pained. They objected to a doctrine according to which man, instead of having been made originally a little lower than the angels, had risen from only a little higher than the beasts of the fields—*instead of being made in the likeness of God, must be regarded rather as having imagined God after his own likeness.* It is true the new doctrine presented man as having risen—and likely therefore to rise still higher—while the old presented him as having fallen grievously, having, from being next door to an angel, and quite in the likeness of God (though, for a slight temptation, or none, held

Every man adores the God whom he has made for
himself in his own image, or has allowed authorities,
who have more or less an interest in his ignorance
and weakness, to impose upon him. To adore
in fear and trembling is almost to *hate*, though
the fear disguises the hate ; to adore fearlessly is
to *love*.

True piety, which is the foundation of religion, is
the exaltation of love, for love raised to a high pitch
admits no longer the barriers of the possible ; the
impossible is its dream, and miracle, for it, reality.
What would avail a religion that did not give us the
infinite ? What is Protestantism with its sacrament
devoid of reality?[1] Sad as an extinguished taper
or a dismantled church ! How can the bread consecrated by the word represent Jesus Christ if it be
not Jesus himself ? What folly if the Christ be not
divinity ! A fine piece of worship, truly, to chew a
mouthful of bread—alas for him who cannot feel the
necessity for miracle here. One can love a human
being to the death, to the forgetfulness of self, to

---

out by an objectionable reptile, he so offended as to
merit death—not, before, a part of the plan), become
a wretched creature, ' deceitful above all things, and
desperately wicked '. So that, on the whole, the
new teaching was a more cheerful one apart from
religious hopes and fears,—which do not belong to
our inquiry here."—*Trans.*

' *i.e.*, in which the bread and wine are not supposed
to be *really* transmuted into Christ's flesh and blood,
as is held by the Romish Church.—*Trans.*

madness, but can one immortalise him and make him
divine, in faith in the making him divine, and immor-
talising oneself along with him ? Can one incorporate
him in oneself ? Eat him altogether and feel that he
lives more than ever, that he lives in us and outside
of us, that he absorbs us in him, as we absorb him in
us, in bringing us into communion with his vast being,
and his eternal love ? Alas ! we feel that he is neither
eternal nor vast ! Why is he not God ? Why, because
God alone is God ! and this is how the God comes to
us, veiled under the appearance of bread! We see
him, we touch him, we taste him, we eat him, and his
eternity trembles within our mortal flesh. The blood
which palpitates in our heart is his. Our bosom
swells, it is he who breathes. Ah ! these Protestants
with their mouthful of bread and sip of wine, truly a
fine Sacrament they have there !

Faith, the poet enamoured of the ideal, smiles at a
ridiculous reality, but the fanatical believer grows
exasperated. Reason says we should pity the Protestants. " No ! " says infuriated Faith, " we must
punish them ! The God which I feel grow wrathful in
me condemns them to hell ; why should I grudge
them to the burning pile ? " Hold, miserable assassin !
Dost thou then believe that God made himself man,
that man might make himself a tiger ? Thou believest
thyself to have conceived with the infinite love, and
behold thou art in labour with hate. Thou hast
thought to devour Heaven and behold thou vomitest
Hell ! Thou hast eaten the flesh of Christ not as a
Christian but as a cannibal. Sacrilegious communicant,

hold thy peace and cleanse thy mouth, for thy lips are dripping with blood.

Doubtless religion must not be held responsible for the crimes which the policy of barbarous ages has committed in her name. Many heretics were at the same time the agents of conspiracies and seditions. The massacre of St. Bartholomew was a cruel *ruse de guerre*, the perfidy of which is perhaps explained by the necessity for rendering abortive a plot not less perfidious.

Thus, at any rate, did the Queen Mother and Charles IX endeavour to justify their action. This at least is certain that, at that period, both parties were capable of any outrage. But what could ever justify the Inquisition ? " God made himself man," it may be replied, and these grand words were understood by Pius V in a terrible, and by Vincent de Paul in an adorable, sense. Did not God, according to the Bible, repent himself of having made man ? Cruel exaggeration of human iniquity ! It is assumed to have been so gigantic as to make God waver in his purpose ! Man divinifies himself even in his crimes, and dreams of opposition to the Eternal. The irreconcileable revolt of the damned and thenceforth the cruelly powerless hate of a God, unable any more to pardon.

Well, even this is sublime in its horror, and the Catholic dogma is admirable even to its most dreadful depths for those souls which realise its poetry without becoming victims of its seductions and its infatuations.

*God appears to repent himself of having made man,
because man from time to time repents himself of
having made a God.* Divine fictions succeed each
other like the ages. Jupiter dethrones Saturn, and
the Jesus Christ of Popes reigns in the place of
Jehovah of the Jews. The Jesus of St. Dominic is
still none the less the son of the cruel God of Moses,
but the ferocious beasts of Daniel and the Apocalypse
must inevitably disappear to make room for the dove
and the lamb. God will truly have made himself
man, when he shall have caused men to become as
good as a God ought to be.[1] The genius of man, in
developing itself in the course of ages, unrolls the
genealogy of the Gods. It is in the genius of man
that an eternal Ancient of Days begets a son that
must succeed to his father · and in which proceeds,
from father and son, the spirit of knowledge and
intelligence which shall explain the mysteries of both.
The Trinity, does not this issue from the very bowels
of humanity ? Does not man feel it to be eternal in
three persons, the father, the mother and the child ?
In the human trinity, is not the son as ancient as the
father ? For the father also is a son ! Is not the

---

[1] That is to say when the Seventh Round men
appear on the scene, then only shall there be a God ;
for the sons of man.—E. O.

For the sons of men yes ; that is to say cognisable
and comprehensible by limited and conditioned in-
tellects ; but this is a different thing from the assertion that there is *no* God, though this latter is, no
doubt, the view taken by E. O.—*Trans.*

woman the immaculate conception of nature and
love ? And this her conception, is it not stainless ?
For the sin of love ends where maternity begins.
There is a virginity in the sanctity of the mother, and
since God has made himself man, that is to say, since
God neither really lives for us, nor personifies himself, nor thinks, nor loves, nor speaks, save only in
humanity, the ideal woman, the typical woman, *the
collective woman, is truly the mother of God.*[1]

―――――――――――――――――――――――――

[1] Woman taken collectively is of course Mother of
God-Humanity, but has Eliphas no other God ? No,
but he has an enemy—Rome. E. L. was an atheist
and a poet. He was also a diplomatist ; he seeks to
win over and not to frighten away his public —E. O.

It is very questionable whether E. L. *was* an
atheist ; indeed it seems to me certain that he was
not. His position was *not* that there was *no* God,
(an assertion involving an assumption of omniscience),
but simply that to the narrow and dim cognisance of man and even to that of far higher but still
conditioned intelligences, God only manifests himself
in Nature and Humanity. To say that the Infinite
and Absolute is entirely outside the highest plane to
which any limited and conditioned intellect can
attain, and that hence we must content ourselves with
dealing with the laws and manifestations of the conditioned Universe, which are more or less within our
grasp or that of our perfected predecessors, is one
thing ; to assert that there *is no* power and intelligence outside the sphere of our possible cognisance,
the source of these laws and manifestations, *no* God
in fact, another, and one to which, to my mind, neither Eliphas Levi, nor any other occultist of his
school, would commit himself.—*Trans.*

There is redemption, that is to say, solidarity amongst men ; the good suffer for the bad, and the just pay the debts of the sinners.[1]   Thus, all is true in the dogmas of religion when once we have the key to the enigma. *Catholicism is the Sphynx of modern times. Place yourself under its talons, without guessing its riddle, and it devours you; guess its riddle without conquering it, or only half guess it, and you are doomed like Œdipus to misfortune and self-imposed blindness.*   An intelligent Catholic ought not to leave the church, he ought to remain in it [2] ; wise amidst the ignorant, free amidst slaves, to enlighten the former and liberate the latter, for I once more repeat that there is no true religion outside the pale of Catholicity.[3]

The rationale of a religion is to be *ir*rational ! Its nature is to be *super*natural.   God is supersubstantial.   Space and the universal substance are the Infinite, God is within it, for he is the knowledge and the power of the infinite.[4]

---

[1] But this is *not* the case in reality, though to a superficial observer it may often seem so.   On the contrary, each and all inevitably pay to the last farthing their own debts (incurred in the current of previous lives) and these only, and pay them either in this or in future lives.—*Trans.*

[2] And that is why E. L. left it—for the sake of a Paradox.—E. O.

[3] A play upon words—Catholicity means with him *Universality.*—E. O.

[4] Our doctrine : Space and Universal *Swābhāvat*— Matter : Force is within.   Manifesting under this

The infinite is the inevitable absurdity which imposes itself on science. God is the paradoxical explanation of the absurdity which imposes itself on faith.

Science and faith can and ought mutually to counterbalance each other and produce equilibrium ; they can never amalgamate.

The eternal Father is Jewish ; the good God is Christian ; the divinity of Jesus Christ, the Pope, and the Devil are Catholic ; but charity, which is Catholic and in a way pre-eminent, will suppress the Devil and convert the idolaters of the Pope.

Original sin is Jewish, pardon is Christian, the sacraments, Catholic.

Fanaticism is of Jewish birth, good sense is Christian, simplicity and intelligence are Catholic, but pretentious folly is Protestant.

Don Juan, Voltaire, the first Napoleon, Venillot, Polichinello, Pierrot and Harlequin are Catholics, but Mons. Prud'homme is Protestant and, what is worse, a Freemason.

Philosophy is Atheistic or Christian, poetry is Catholic, and egotistic and mercantile jejuneness are Protestant.

This is why France is Voltairean, but still Catholic, whereas the English, the Prussians and M.* * * are Protestants.

Trinitarian form, a God, for the ignorant and the blind.—E. O.

"Yes, gentlemen of the Ecclesiastical Hierarchy," said the Catholic Galileo, "the Earth is fixed, if you desire it; it is the Sun which revolves. I will say more if you demand it, I will say that the earth is flat and the Heavens made of crystal. Would to God that your skulls were of the same material so as to allow a little light to penetrate to your respected brains. You are authority, and science is bound to bow; she can afford to bow when she meets you, for it is she who remains, you who pass away. Your successors will e'en be forced in their turn to bow to and live in peace with her."

Rabelais, not less learned and not less a good Catholic than Galileo, wrote the following in the prologue of his fourth book of *Gargantua* :

" If in my life, my writings, my speech, nay even in my thoughts, I detected the faintest glimmer of heresy, with my own hands should the dry wood be collected and the fire kindled to burn myself on the pile."

Do you see here Rabelais, the inquisitor, burning himself, Rabelais, accused of heresy ?

This reminds one of *God, causing God to die in order to appease God.* It is inexplicable, as a mystery should be, but it is only the more essentially Catholic.

Nothing so excites the imagination as mystery, and the excited imagination electrifies and multiplies tenfold the will. The wise are called to govern the world, but it is the mad men who overturn and metamorphose it. This is why madness is considered by Eastern nations as something divine. Indeed to

vulgar eyes the man of genius is a mad man. In
truth, he has, perhaps, some grains of madness in
him, for he almost always disregards common sense
to obey the sublime sense. Moses dreams of a Promised Land and drags away into the desert a horde
of herdsmen and slaves, who murmur, rebel, kill each
other and die of hunger and fatigue during forty
years. He will never reach Palestine ; he will die,
lost in the mountain, but his thought will have swept
the heavens, and he will bequeath to the world a God,
unique, and an universal code; from the shade of
Moses, unburied, will issue the immeasurable glory
of Jehovah.

He created a people and commenced a book ; a
people, bravely mean in its tenacity, at once superb
and servile ; a book, full of shadows and lights, of
a grandeur and absurdity alike superhuman ; this
book and this people will withstand all force, all
science, all political combinations, and all the criti-
cisms of the nations and the revolving ages. From
this book civilisation will derive its worship, from this
people kings will borrow their treasures, and who now
will dare to judge the man of the Red Sea and Mount
Horeb ? What rationalistic philosopher can think
that he was wise ? But who, capable of appreciating
great things, could dare to call him foolish ?

Shall we speak now of Jesus Christ ? But here we
should bow before him whom half the world adores.
What great hierophant, what ancient oracle could ever
have foreseen this God ? What astrologer, or what
Diviner could have conceived the idea of saying to

the Emperor Tiberius : " At this moment a Jew of
Galilee, proscribed by his own people, denied by his
friends, and condemned by one of your Prefects, is
dying in agony. After his death he will dethrone
the Cæsars, and those who will claim to continue his
inconceivable dynasty will reign in Rome in your
place. All the Gods of the Empire and of the entire
world will fall before his image ; the instrument of
his punishment will become the symbol of Salvation."
What madness is Christianity if it be not superhuman ! What an awful faith, that in Jesus Christ,
if he be not God !¹ Can you conceive a mental
disease, contagious enough to infect with delirium
through a long series of centuries almost the whole of
humanity ? What a deluge of blood has that
abolisher of bloody sacrifices caused to flow ! What
implacable hatreds, what vengeance, what wars, what
tortures, what massacres, has not this promulgator
of pardon excited ? But Jesus was more than a man ;
he was an idea, nay more than an idea, a principle ;
I am a principle that speaks, said he, speaking of
himself.

God has made himself man ; thus is proclaimed
upon earth the worship of humanity. " *Emmanuel*

---

¹ " Now the Virgin returns, the golden age returns,
Now a new offspring is sent down from high Heaven,
O Chaste Lucina, favour the boy now being born,
The serpent will die."—*Virgil's 4th Eclogue.*

Virgil died September 22nd, 19 B.C. Was he a
Prophet ?—E. O.

God is in us," *would say as they embraced each*
other the Brothers of the Rosy Cross, initiated in the
mystery of the Man-God.[1] For truly the Son of
Man is at the same time the only and multiple Son
of God.[2] You are one with me, said the Master to
his disciples, as my Father and I are one ; he who
hears you hears me, and he who sees me, sees my
Father. Triumph and miracle ! God is no longer
unknown to men, because man knows man. He is no
longer invisible when we see our neighbour. He is
the benefactor who assists *us*, He is the poor man
whom *we* assist, He is the sick who suffers, the
physician who heals. He is the sufferer who weeps
and the friend who consoles. And woman,—how
Christianity elevates her ! What an assumption is
hers ; the woman is the mother of God since God
has made himself man ! A virgin—we can love her
with all our aspirations to infinity ; a mother—but it
is no longer sufficient to love her, we must adore
her as we adore Grace and Providence. The law of
pardon on her lips, she is peace and mercy, she is
nature and life, she is obedience—free, and Liberty
—self-submitting. She is *all* that we should love !
Recite in her honour the Litanies of the Virgin-
Mother ; I salute you, Gate of Heaven, Temple of
Ivory, Sanctuary of Gold, Mysterious Rose, Sacred

---

[1] " Man is God and Son of God, and there is no
other God but man." (The secret pledge of the
Rosicrucians).—E. O.

[2] " Humanity—Son of Eternity."—E. O.

Vase of Devotion, Honourable Vase, Admirable Vase,
Pyxis of Love, Cup of Holy Desires,¹ Star of the
Morning, Arch of the Alliance.

Oh ! what cries of love do all those *martyrs, self-
condemned to eternal widowhood*, raise, *without
comprehending them*, to thee ! Oh cruel, despairing
sigh of all these Tantaluses thirsting for a draught
that ever eludes them, and provoked to longings
by fruits ever denied to their lips. Sublime
dreamers ! They renounce woman to gain heaven,
as if heaven was something without woman, and as if
woman was not the Queen of Heaven ! " O trespass
of Adam, happy trespass," sings the Church in her
liturgy, " happy trespass which has deserved to have
God himself as its redeemer ! O sin of Adam, sin
truly inevitable ! " Thus escape in the sacred chants
the innermost secrets of the Sanctuary, but those who
repeat these mysterious words fail to catch their true
sense, and their hearts, burning perhaps beneath the
ashes, accuse themselves of a desire, as though it
were a shame, and of a regret, as though it were an
infidelity !

Religion then is the exaltation of the man and
the assumption of the woman. Comprehension of
religion is the emancipation of the spirit, and the

---

¹ Compare these expressions taken from the
litanies of the R. C. Church with like sexual flatteries
addressed to Durga's idol (the *Yoni*) by Hindu
devotees and the litanies of the Vallabacharyas to
the God of Love.—E. O.

Bible of the hierophants *is the Bible of liberty.* To believe without knowing is weakness; *to believe, because one knows, is power.*

Paradox II.—Liberty is Obedience to the Law

WHERE there is the spirit of God there is Liberty, say the Holy Scriptures.

Ye shall know the truth, and the truth shall make you free, said Jesus Christ.   We should escape from the bondage of the letter to the liberty of the spirit, said the great Apostle.[1]   Also he says, you have been

---

[1] The Deity is semi-male (? Hermaphrodite.— *Trans.*) in the Hebrew philosophy.   The body of man is the vehicle of the three pairs of spouses, viz., the 2nd and 3rd, the 4th and 5th, and the 6th and 7th principles.

Irenæus speaks of " Bathos and Sige, Mind and Aletheia," each of them male and female.   The three *pairs* of principles are then treated as three only, and we have the Trinity.   The Jewish Kabala gives Macroprosopus his spouse, and the Microprosopus his *uxor.*   (Liber Mysteri, I, 35, 38.)

" The anointed they call, male—female," says Cyril of Jerusalem, VI, xi. The SUN has the Pneuma for his spouse.

When Eliphas Levi speaks of Christ and his church, he means the Monad and its vehicle, the 7th and 6th principles.   The Egyptian older Hermetic books give the first Quaternation, Monotes (Proarche, Proanennoetos, Mysterious and not to be named says

bought for a great price, do not any more make
yourselves slaves of men. We are the children and
not the slaves of God. We are the brothers and not
the slaves of Jesus Christ.

The law was made for man and not man for the
law, said again, the Divine Master. Liberty is the
goal of man's existence ; it is in this alone that his
right and his duty can be reconciled ; in this consists
his personality and autonomy, and this alone can
render him capable and worthy of Immortality.

Irenæus) and Henotes, the power that exists in union
with "the Lord Ferho, the unknown, formless, unconscious Life " of the Codex Nazaræus.

This Monotes and Henotes, being the ONE, *sent
forth*, not produced, but unconsciously emanated, a
BEGINNING, as they call it (*arche*), before all things
Intelligible, Unborn and Invisible, which *arche* is the
MONAD (from the ONE).

In the West the religious philosophy of the Magi
was first made famous under the name of Oriental
Wisdom. Simon Magus teaches the doctrine of the
Father, Son and Holy Spirit (*female*), and says that
this Trinity had appeared amongst the Jews as Son,
amongst the Samaritans as Father, and to other
nations as the Holy Spirit. The Christian Trinity
was bodily taken from the Kabalistic Nazarenes, who
existed ages before the Western Christ, and to whom
Jeshu (the Jesus of Lud, 13o B.C. ?) belonged during
the period of Alexander Jannæus (*a*).

" Life has built the house (body) in which you now
stay, and the seven planets who dwell in it shall
not ascend all into the land of Light.—" *Codex
Naz.*, II, 35.

*To free ourselves from the slavery of the Passions,
from the tyranny of Prejudices, from the errors of
Ignorance, the pains of Fear, and the anxieties of
Desire,* this is the Work of Life.

It is a question of being or not being. The free
man is alone a man; slaves are but animals or
children.

St. Augustine sums up the whole law in this fine
saying: "Love, and do what you like."[1]

The free man can wish nothing but what is good,
for all wicked men are slaves.

Following the spirit of our (*Catholic*) symbols, the
freedom of man is God's great work; for this he
permits a Hell to be hollowed out, and the hideous
shadow of the Demon to be raised even to Heaven.
It is for this that to the more than regal quietude of
Divinity he prefers the sufferings of the accursed
Humanity. God aspires to the cross of the malefactor

"Yes! the Chaldeans call the God. IAO, SABAOTH,
he who is over the SEVEN Orbits (circles)—the
Demiurge."—*Lydus de Mens*, IV, 38, 74. The seven
orbits are the seven principles, the three couples with
the house of flesh.

"Beam of the sun that hath shone the fairest light
of all before the *Seven*-gated Thebes, thou hast at
length gleamed forth, O eye of golden Day."—Sopho-
cles, *Antigone.*—E. O.

(*a*) Alexander Jannæus is generally reckoned as
reigning from 106 or 104 B.C. to 79 B.C.—*Trans.*

[1] But adds in so many words: "Provided that you
do nothing contrary to the commandments of the
Church."—E. O.

and wills, so as not to be a despot abusing Omnipotence, to conquer, by suffering, the right to pardon rebellion. The woman has been audacious, she has desired to know ; the man has been sublime, he has dared to love; and God, who while admiring strikes them, seems to have become jealous of the patience of his children.

All this is a revelation, poetic and esoteric ; all this has occurred in the Human mind and in the Human heart. Man feels his high dignity when he wills to be free ; the eternal vulture may tear the liver of Prometheus, but the courage of the great sufferer is reborn and grows ever with his daring. Jupiter avenges himself, but fears, and *he* will dethrone Jupiter and prove himself more a God than him, who will give his whole heart's blood to heal the wounds of Prometheus, and will come to suffer in his place.

Emancipation, Liberty, this is the final word of the Symbols. Jesus descended to Hell to kill the slavery of Death, and in re-ascending towards the light he dragged after him captivity, captive.

One day, Death alone will be dead ; Curses alone will be accursed, and Damnation alone damned, and the Spirit of Light which desires that all men should be saved, all arrive at a knowledge of the truth, God —who after having made all human beings *en masse* responsible for the fault of a single one, may well pardon all on account of the merits of one—God will cause good to triumph, and evil will be destroyed.

The time will come when it will be realised that there is no true Liberty without Religion, no true

Religion without Liberty, but at present Religion and
Liberty seem mutually to exclude and battle against
each other. Like Religion, Liberty has her martyrs,
and Liberty will deny authority so long as the Church
denies the rights of Liberty.

" Ought we to concede to men the liberty of conscience ? " asked our Doctors, and Rome decided in
the negative, but that simply means that the Church
does not renounce the direction of those who listen
to her.

Liberty is not given, she is seized, or rather Nature
gives her to us by the help of science ; to ask whether
one should allow to men, true men, the Liberty of
conscience, is as if one asked whether we should allow
them a head and a heart. Did not Galileo, even after
he had withdrawn his learned demonstrations, know
that the earth revolved ? Will civilisation turn backwards, because there is a syllabus ? Should the Pope
forbid us to proceed ? Let us salute the Pope and
move on always. If the Holy Father wishes to make
us hear him, he must e'en move on in his turn ; it is
full time for the shepherd to rise when his flock goes
off. Hold ! some one will say, your position as a
Catholic does not permit you to speak thus.

If legitimate authority imposes silence on me I
hold my tongue, *but* the earth revolves !

Conscience is inviolable, for it is divine, and it
is in truth that which is essentially and absolutely
free in man. For outside the conscience where can
one find an absolute realisation of that ideal—
Liberty ?

21

From his cradle man is subjected to tyrannical
necessities, and, like it or no, as he may, he must
bear throughout his life that chain of obligations
which society and nature emulate each other in imposing on him. Truth and Justice are austere mistresses,
and Love is a despot, often cruel. For him who is
not rich come the necessities of existence ; there is no
alternative between the yoke of labour and the work
pillar [1] of misery. Those who are called the masters
and the happy ones of the world have other enemies
and other chains ; so true is this that Alexander the
Great almost envied the cynical half madness and
indifference of Diogenes ; but Diogenes and Alexander
were the two extremes of paradoxical vanity ; they
were both the slaves of their Pride, and were not free
men.

Liberty is the full enjoyment of all those rights
which do not connote a duty. It is by the accom-
plishment of duty that rights are acquired and
preserved. Man has the right to do his duty because
he is bound to preserve his rights. Self-devotion is
only a sublimation of duty, and it is the most sublime
of all rights. A man may devote himself to another,
but that is not being his slave; he may pawn his
liberty, but he cannot alienate it without a species of
moral suicide. A man may devote his life to the

[1] "*Ergastule.*" I never before met the word in
French, but I take it to be derived from *ergastylos*,
the pillar to which a recusant slave was chained to
work ; also the beams to which slaves in galleys were
chained to row.—*Trans.*

triumph of an idea, but always reserving the right of mental expansion and to a devotion to a worthier object. *A perpetual vow is an affirmation of the Absolute in the Relative, of Knowledge in Ignorance, of the Immutable in the Transitory, of Contradiction in all things.* It is, therefore, an engagement, null and void, because it is rash and absurd and to repent (and withdraw from it) when one realises its madness, is not merely a right, but a duty.

It is true that the Church, whose decisions in matters of Faith ought to be respected by all Catholics, approves perpetual vows ; but this is solely when they are the result of a supernatural grace.[1] Such vows are void before nature, but in the supernatural order they are sacred and inviolable.[2]

Marriage also is a perpetual engagement that nature does not always ratify. Thence follow alike the just but useless severities of morality and the deterioration of manners. Thence follow in perpetual contrast the tears and blood of the conjugal tragedy, and the inexhaustible merriment of tales and comedy. Moses is terrible when he descends from Mount Sinai with horns; but why had he horns ? Because he was a married man,[3] will perhaps reply some unblushing

---

[1] Or of a determined desire to obtain a supernatural power. To command nature it is necessary to be positive. She has no obedience for mixed magnetisms.—E. O.

[2] True.—E. O.

[3] Behold a Frenchman ! cynical and witty, even in the midst of the arduous discussion of esoteric

Gaul, and because he had absented himself for forty nights from the conjugal couch! The old joke spares nothing.

The two greatest free-thinkers the world has known were Rabelais and Lafontaine, those two past Masters in wit and humour.[1] Both of them, moreover, good Catholics and free from any suspicion of heresy. Rabelais had taken religious vows and had the cleverness to make himself tolerated by the Pope. Lafontaine was married, and did not live with his wife; but what magicians of style! What apostles of the pure frank Truth! The work of Rabelais is the Bible of good sense and infallible gaiety; that of Lafontaine is the Evangel of Nature. Rabelais used to say mass, and if Lafontaine had lived in his time he doubtless would not have failed to assist in this by reading the prophecies of Baruch.

One ought to do what one likes, when one likes what one ought. This is the Law of Liberty! In other words, every man has the right to do his duty, but the first duty of man is set forth in the first commandment of the Decalogue.

---

philosophy. France has had several renowned Alchemists, she never had *one true Adept.*—E. O.

[1] It is impossible to translate adequately the original word "*gauloiserie*," with its double meaning and wide reaching significations. It is what Humpty Dumpty would have called a "portmanteau word".—*Trans.*

Thou shalt worship one God only, and him only shalt thou obey.[1]

And Jesus amplifying this precept, to the point of giving his explanation a paradoxical character, did not hesitate to add : You shall call no one in this world master or father ; one only is your father, your master, and that is God.[2]

And St. John, the intimate confidant of the thoughts of Jesus, tells us that God is the Word, or Reason, " and the Word was God."

Therefore we have and we ought to have for master only Reason, or the Word which speaks.

For the Word, adds St. John, " was the true Light which lighteth every man that cometh into the world."

Jesus Christ said of himself : I am the principle that speaks.[3]

And every man who speaks in accordance with Reason can say, " I am Reason." And one ought to do and avoid what it prescribes, for the Will of Reason prevails over the Caprice of man. Caprice is the choice of amusements. One may pick and

---

[1] In the Massoretic Kabala, the *points* read : " One God, only—the TRUTH,—and her only shalt thou obey." Having so much of the Jesuit in him, E. L. could never become an adept.—E. O.

[2] God, or *Good*.—E. O.

[3] In this and many other cases, the *wording* of the authorised English version differs. But the sense is generally the same.—*Trans.*

choose where amusements are concerned, but not in
the case of duty that imposes itself on us, and we are
compelled to accept and do it.

Duty crushes him who seeks to avoid it, but bears
onward with love him who accomplishes it.

To will what we ought, that is to will what God [1]
wills. And when the will of man is the same as the
divine will,[2] it becomes omnipotent.

Then it is that the miracles of Faith are accomplished ; then may we command the mountains to be
moved, and the fruit trees to transplant themselves
into the sea—words of our Saviour which are not to
be taken in their literal sense.

The Word of Reason is efficacious, because it wills
the end, and determines the means.

It is certain that neither the mountains nor the
trees will remove themselves of their own accord.

The Force manipulates the Matter, and the
Thought directs the Force.

Faith avails itself of Knowledge, and Knowledge
directs Faith.

God himself can do nothing in opposition to Reason, which is the Law of Justice, because Justice,
Law and Reason are God himself.

God does not arrest the sun and moon, to allow
Joshua to slay certain Canaanites, and the announce-
ment of such a miracle can only be a hyperbolical
figure of speech of Oriental poetry.

---

[1] Or what Truth and Duty will.—E. O.
[2] Will—the Ākāsic Force.—E. O.

God does not reject a people after having chosen
it, and he does not change his religion after having
given it as eternal.

Arbitrary commands, favours, privileges, wrath, re-
pudiation, pardon, belong only to the weakness of man.

But to make children gradually understand Reason,
it is needful sometimes to throw over it an appearance
of folly.

Childhood is naturally foolish; it must have its
absurd stories and its sensational toys. It must have
its automatic dolls, its animals moving by mechanism.
It is true that it will very soon break these to see what
is inside them.

And thus Humanity breaks one after the other all
its childish Religions.

The true Religion is the eternal Religion.

The true Piety is the Piety that is independent.
The true Faith is the absolute Faith which explains
all Symbols and moves above all Dogmas. The true
God is the God of Reason, and his true worship is
Love and Liberty.

The Christians were right in breaking the idols,
because men insisted on forcing *them* to adore these.
The Protestants were right in trampling under foot,
and burning the images of the Saints because, to
compel them to worship these, men burnt the Protestants themselves.

Nevertheless what more Divine than the great
works of Phidias and the Virgins of Raphael?

The worship of images, is it not the worship of Art,
and was not the beautiful Religion of the Greeks one

of the most graceful and splendid forms of the
Universal Religion ?

I adore truly the Divine Majesty before the Jupiter
of Phidias, Immortal Beauty in the Venus of Milo,
the Divinity of Man in the Christ of Michelangelo, the
Dream of Heaven in the paradise of Fra Angelico.

But if to compel me to the worship of one or other
of these, you show me scaffolds or blazing piles. . . .
I would despise the executioner and turn my back on
the idol !

Oh Madness of Human Tyranny !

In France, in the very country whose name even
signifies Liberty, they raised scaffolds before the idol
of Liberty herself.

Yet Robespierre and Marat cursed the Inquisitors
as the Inquisitors had cursed Nero and Diocletian,
and Marat and Robespierre have been cursed in their
turn by later assassins, and Liberty still remains a
gory Paradox, an Idol demanding sacrifices.

To this day the world has continued a great mad-
house. Numbers have seized one, saying to him,
" Worship my slipper, or I burn you ! "

If the man who fell into their claws was cunning,
he made believe to worship the slipper, and perhaps in
so doing was neither a hypocrite nor an idolater,[1] but
their victim is a guileless fellow, who takes the thing,
in sad earnest, resists them, and becomes a Martyr !

The lassitude that succeeds to debauchery drives
men to the madness of suicide, and the orgies of the

---

[1] Only a worthy son of Loyola !—E. O.

Decadence were bound to end fatally in the epidemic of Martyrdom. Young girls in those days skipped to the burning pile as to a dance ; infatuated mothers dragged their infants to the massacre. Executioners, tired of slaying, flung down their axes and begged for death. " Take off your neck-ruffs," wrote Tertullian to the Christian women, " and make room for the sabre of the executioners." Children played at Martyrdom, and one was seen red-heating fragments of iron to place upon his hand. The Roman cruelty provoked a reaction, and the taste for torture as an exhibition created a desire to experience it as a new sensation.

Polygnotus and Nearchus, interrupting a religious ceremony and overthrowing the altars of the Father-land before a horrified people, do they seem to have acted as reasonable beings ? What then ? Did not St. Paul premise the folly of the cross ? And Jesus himself, did he not make a disturbance in the Temple of Jerusalem ? He was God, you will tell me. So be it, but humanly speaking his conduct was extreme-ly irregular and very imprudent, and you would agree with me on this point . . . *if* you dared.

Is it lawful under the pretext that one is a God to be less prudent than a wise man ? This is what one has, if not the right, at least the inclination to inquire ; at least if one accepted the Gospels as his-tory. But they are more than this ; they are precepts and symbols. God disapproves of commerce in Holy things ; he will not have traffic in his Temple, and the sellers deserve to be driven thence with blows of scourges ; their shops should be overthrown, their money trampled under foot. This is all that the Legend (or if you will the Holy Evangel) of the sellers driven from the Temple signifies ; here I bow and hold my peace.[1]

All is beautiful in our Religion when one knows how to understand it. All our Religion is true, and I would even dare to say that every Religion is true, apart from omissions, transpositions, wrong meanings, rash conjectures, additions, imaginings and misunderstandings.

This is what the free-thinkers must at last realise if they do not desire to be for ever battling against one of the most energetic forces of Human Nature, the invincible want to believe in, and adore something in the Infinite, and to have Faith in a Humanity greater in some respect than nature, so as to rise ever towards this, and to become purer in it, in order to conquer and to reign by it.

Voltaire did not desire to destroy Religion, but he wished to reduce it to a pure Deism. His motto was : " *God and Liberty.*" He, who fancied himself a Poet, and yet understood nothing of the great Epic Poem of the Symbols, which starts from blind [2] Forces to

---

[1] Instead of canonising, the Church of Rome unfrocked and persecuted to his death poor Eliphas, the Abbé Louis Constant. " It is dangerous to leave things half undone," confessed the man when dying.—E. O.

[2] In the original, "*forces fatales,*" by which I take it he means not merely " fatal forces," but the blind,

arrive at Intelligence and Liberty, stamps on suns, the sacred fire of Zoroaster, allows its robbery by Prometheus in defiance of the bolts of Jove, adores the force which it enchains at the feet of Beauty, traverses the splendid and almost infinite domain of glorious dreams, and finally accomplishes its synthesis in the reality of Man.

God is no longer the giant, invisible, fantastic. solitary, hidden in the unfathomable depths of Heaven, He is amongst us, he is in us, he has been born of the Woman, he is a babe whose new born cries we hear, a youth who thinks and loves, an outlaw who struggles and suffers, a free-thinker who protests, a reformer who drives out the buyers and sellers from the Holy Place, one accursed who blesses, and rises from the dead, the pure Man who pardons the adulterous Woman, the physician who heals, but also the sick man who hopes, the paralytic who arises and walks, the blind who opens his eyes. The others are me, said the Saviour, and he who sees me, sees also my Father ; all that is done to the least of these is done to me, and God is in me, as I am in Him. Does He speak only of the chosen people of the blessed race of Abraham ? No ! for He blesses equally the good Samaritan, the Centurion, the woman of Canaan, and the immense herd of nations whom He hopes to gather into one fold. So he who gives bread to the poor,

---

unintelligent forces of the universe, that work on, slaves to the inherent laws of their being, and irresistible tyrants to all who have not pierced their secret.—*Trans.*

gives bread to God; he who consoles a sufferer,
consoles God; he who blesses an infidel, blesses God;
he who injures one man, injures God; he who curses
one man, curses God; he who slays one man, commits
Deicide.

What would Jesus have thought of the pitiless
Priest and Levite excommunicating and condemning
to death the good Samaritan as a schismatic, and the
wounded man of Jericho for having received with
gratitude the help and care of an infidel? What
must his judgment be on those Inquisitors who have
imprisoned, tortured, and burnt God alive? But the
God of these men was the Devil, and their Religion
was that of Anti-Christ. Man has no right to kill
man, except in self-defence.[1] The execution of a
criminal is a misfortune of war in a Society which is

---

[1] And not even then, for where would be the difference between the two?—E. O.
The difference would be that the one seeks to
kill, in violation of his neighbour's right to live,
aggressively, and not in defence of his own inherent right, whilst the other if he does also infringe his neighbour's right to kill, does so only
defensively in vindication of his own inherent right to
live. There is a broad distinction between the two
cases that no sophistry can level; both *may* be wrong,
but even so (a moot point with the highest moralists
of all ages) there is a vast difference in the degree of
criminality in the two cases. E. O. condemns suicide
unconditionally, and rightly so, but to allow a man
to kill you, when you can prevent this by killing
him, is, it seems to me, suicide to all intents and
purposes.—*Trans.*

not yet Christian, but the executed one who accepts
the expiation is the Father of the good thief dying
on the cross with the Saviour, and we must see in
him God severing himself from the brute.   Crime is
not a human act, but sacrifice is Divine when it is
voluntary.   *Homo sum humani a me nil alienum
puto.*   I am a man, and nothing human can be foreign
to me.   This is what God has said to the world in
the Spirit of the Christian Revelation.

*Let us seek God in Nature, let us worship Him in
Spirit and in Truth, let us love and serve Him in
Humanity.   That is Religion, eternal and definitive.*[2]

And when the chief of the Human Family have
entered on this path, we shall be able to say with
Voltaire : " God is Liberty," *for man will understand God, and will deserve to be free.*

Paradox III.—Love is the Realisation

of the Impossible

Love is the Omnipotence of the Ideal.   By the Ideal
the soul is exalted ; it becomes greater than Nature,
more living than the world, loftier than Science,
more immortal than Life.

When Jesus Christ said : Love God with all your
heart and your neighbour as yourself, this is the Law

----

[1] Only whatever we do let us call things by their
right names, " *Pas de demi-inconnues.*"—E. O.

and the Prophets, he intended to signify : Love, Love, above everything ; for God is infinite Love ; further, love your neighbour as yourself, that is to say, love yourself in your neighbour.

Egoism if properly ordered commences with others.[1]

To love is to live, to love is to know, to love is to be able, to love is to pray, to love is to be the Man-God.

The woman dared to ruin herself, in order to pluck Divinity and offer it to Man, and Man, who had no thirst for Divinity, for he had Woman, the Man took it as a simple thing to follow his companion to death.

There commenced the incarnation of God. Eve compelled God to make himself man, for she had become a mother.

*　　　*　　　*　　　*　　　*

Death and Hell had reared themselves, terrible with eternal menace, and one instant of Love had vanquished them.

Love is stronger than Death, says the Song of Songs. It is more insurmountable than Hell. Love is the Eternal Fire, and there is no Deluge which can extinguish this.

Give for a little Love all that you have, all that you hope for, all you value, and all you are. Your

---

[1] In other words Altruism is the highest form of Egoism.—*Trans.*

3

blood, your heart, your life and your soul, and you will·have purchased it for—nothing !

He who would save his soul from Love shall lose his soul, and he who would lose his soul for Love, shall save it.

Many sins shall be forgiven to the heart that has loved much ; it is Jesus Christ himself who said it.

And he had as a companion and friend the Magdalene, and he asked for water to drink from the woman of Samaria, a sinner, and he pardoned the woman taken in adultery, and he said that loose women would enter into Heaven before Pharisees and Doctors of the Law, because the errors of Love are more excusable than those of Pride, because it is better even to love wrongly, than not to love at all.

In Absolute Morality, Good is Love ; Evil is Hate. Love must be loved and only Hate hated. One single word of Hate, say the Gospels, deserves Hell, and consequently one word of Love merits Heaven twice over, for Love rewards even more liberally than Hate punishes.

But is not Love itself its own reward ? He who loves, has he not found the key of Heaven ?

To St. Teresa, the ideal of hell was the impossibility of loving, and this seemed to her so dreadful that she pitied Satan. " The unhappy one," she used to say, " he can no longer love."

The woman pitied the Demon, what a reform of Christianity !

When the world shall have learnt to love, the world will be saved.[1]

The man who knows how to love attracts to himself all souls.

To covet is not to love. To exact is not to love. To enslave is not to love.

Jealousy is the egoism which assumes the mask of love.

Excessive desire produces disgust ; exactingness merits denial.

Tyranny excites rebellion in the strong and treachery in the weak.

Jealousy is odious and ridiculous. To hate the heart that no longer loves us, is it not to punish it for *having* loved us ?

Jealous fury is furious ingratitude.

But there is a sublime jealousy, which is but the zeal of love, and which for the honour of Love itself desires the honour of the beloved. For the beloved is ever the supreme Ideal of the Soul, it is the mirage of the Absolute.

---

[1] That is to say when love of self shall have given place to love of neighbour and of *all* neighbours.—E. O.

There is a terrible apparent confusion in many passages of this discourse between that love which is of the spirit, and that which is of the flesh ; the Divine and earthly, the love which is animal egoism, and that which is the highest form of altruism. But it is more apparent than real as will be seen later on.— *Trans.*

Likings and passing fancies are not Love.

True Love is the apprehension of God in man ; it is the essence of religion, of honour, of friendship and of marriage.

Not only is Love immortal, but it is Love which makes the soul immortal. It ages not, neither does it change. Hearts may turn away from it as the earth turns away from the sun when she would sleep, and it is then that the coldness of night seems to fall upon the soul.

In the physical plane Love is the principle of life : in the spiritual or metaphysical plane, it is the principle of Immortality.

Re-ascending to the origin of all things and diffusing itself thence over all beings, it is called Piety, Charity, and goodness ; when it compels respect for duty it is called Honour : it is the mainspring of Human Individuality.

Manifestly it is immortal, for it yields nothing to Death ; it braves him, despises him and often makes of him a blessing and a glory ; what is a martyr but a witness who affirms the Life Eternal despite tortures and death ?

Love affirms itself absolutely ; where Love is, there Fear is not. It imposes its own conditions on life, and cannot be conditioned by her.

Love must be free in man : in Nature it is the child of Destiny.[1]   Like the magnet, it has two forces ;

---

[1] Here again I can find no translation for the word " *fatal* " which, as contrasted with " *libre*," means

it attracts and repels, it creates and it destroys. It is the brother of Death, but it is the elder brother. It is the God of whom Death is the priest, the God who brightens Death with his beauty, while Death glorifies him by eternal sacrifices.

It has a shadow that men call Hate, and this shadow is needed to show forth its splendour.

Beauty is its smile, happiness its joy, deformity its sorrow, and pain its proof.

War is its fierce fever ; the Passions, its diseases ; Wisdom, its triumph and repose.

It is blind, but it carries a torch ; it is Lucifer, Angel and Demon, it is Damnation and Salvation.

It is Eros equilibrised by Anteros ; it is St. Michael standing on Satan as a pedestal.

The grand arcanum of Magic is the mystery of Love.

Love causes Angels to die and immortalises Demons.

It changes into women the Sylphs, Undines and Gnomes, and draws the elementaries ¹ down to earth.

Love has promised Pandora to Prometheus ; it is for Pandora that the heart of Prometheus ceaselessly re-grows beneath the vulture's talons, and for Prometheus that Pandora still guards Hope.

Heaven is a song of Love fulfilled ; Hell, a roar of Love deceived ; but, as has said a great Poet, the

---

the result of fate ; a thing that takes place without the option of intelligence—a blind result of blind, unintelligent, irresistible forces.—*Trans.*

¹ *Eggrégons*, in the original.—*Trans.*

shadows of Hell are visible darknesses, since there is always some light in the night.

If Hell had not a valid cause of existence in Love, it would be the crime of God.

Hell is the laboratory of Redemption, and it is eternal, so that the work of reparation may be eternal, for God has always been, and always will be, what he is.

Eternal suffering is the cry of the eternal bringing forth.

At the foot of the Saviour's cross, in evangelical representations, appear two women. One stands erect and veiled, motionless and pale as a statue in the majesty of her grief ; this, the Virgin without stain, the mother who conceived without sin. The other, prostrate and wailing, her hair and garments in wild disorder, her eyes red with weeping, her bosom heaving with sobs : this is the sinner, Mary Magdalene, reprobated by the world, blessed by him who dies.

On either side of Christ two men writhe in agony, two malefactors—the one repentant, the other hardened.

To the one Jesus said, I pardon thee, but to the other he did *not* say, I condemn thee, but he suffered in silence *with* him and for him.

Irrevocable damnation is the eternal reprobation of Hate ; the irremediable suffering of the being who will never love.

Involuntary Love is not a sentiment peculiarly human ; it is the universal instinct of all Nature.

The animal makes no choice of allurements ; man alone holds in his hand this golden apple destined by Heaven for the most beautiful. Would he be wise, he will choose Minerva; would he have power, Juno will be his choice ; but if the gratification of the senses suffice him, it will be to Venus that he will offer the apple.

This did the poltroon Paris. Agamemnon would have chosen Juno, and was assassinated by Clytemnestra. Ulysses admired only Minerva ; so had he Penelope as spouse, so triumphed he over the Sirens, over Calypso and Circe, escaped from Polyphemus and Neptune, trampled beneath his feet his enemies and rivals, and thus reconquered his nuptial couch and his throne.

The poems of Homer are divine teachings, whose characters are types. Agamemnon and the two Ajaxes are the triple pride of Power, of Valour and of Rebellion. Achilles is Wrath, Paris is Pleasure, Nestor is the Experience that speaks, Ulysses is the Intelligence that acts. His labours are the trials of the initiation, corresponding with those of Hercules, but Hercules succumbed to a fatal Love, and died the victim of Deianeira. Ulysses enjoys possession of Calypso and Circe without allowing them to possess him; he loves what he ought, and what he wills to love ; his country is his spouse, and this single-hearted love bears him victorious through all.

Love is the greatest power of man, when it is not the most unworthy weakness. He is weak if an ego-tist ; he is strong if he is self-devoted. Hercules buys

at the feet of Omphale the voluptuous joys of which
he is the slave. With his eyes, his honour, and his
liberty, Samson pays for the treacherous kisses of
Delilah ; Orpheus must not glance at Eurydice if he
would tear her from the grasp of Hell ; conquered by
the thirst for that beauty which he yearns to look
upon once more, he turns, and all is over—never will
he look on her again.

It is that the true Love binds himself not to the
beauty which passes away ; beauty for him is eternal,
and can escape him never, since he is strong enough
to create her. The sage loves not a woman because
she is beautiful ; he holds her beautiful because he
loves her, and because he has good reason to love her.

Animal love is of evil omen. Human love is a providence. Ulysses in the arms of Calypso and Circe
was not unfaithful to Penelope, because his only
thought was how to escape from them to rejoin his
wife ; he sinned only against the delicacies of love,
and he will be punished for it by the son of Circe.
The grain of illegitimate children is the seed of
parricides.

When there is not the faith, or at least illusion and
the desire of eternity, sexual love is a glutting of
animality or a fantasy of debauch. Lechery is a
desecration of love that nature punishes and wounded
love avenges. Sooner or later Don Juan must meet
the terrible statue of the commander. But can we
always preserve ourselves from this ill-omened love ?
Can we irrevocably devote the heart to love the free
and the legitimate ?

We can, by knowledge and by will; when we *know* what we ought to will, then we love what we ought to love.

Paradox IV.—Knowledge is the Ignorance or Negation of Evil

" Father, forgive them, for they know not what they do," said Christ, in praying for his executioners.

Thus speaking, he was pleading the cause of all Humanity. All men deceive themselves because " they know not," and no man knows *what* he does when he does evil. How could a rational being with a perfect discernment do evil?[1] Does any one voluntarily take poisons for perfumes, gall for honey, hemlock for parsley, or arsenic for salt?

Ignorance is the cause of all errors, of all crimes and of all the evils that torment the Human Race.

It was ignorance that invented capricious and angry Gods; it was this that foisted on God the worst passions of man; it was this that constructed out of the intelligent principle of things a personality, distinct, defined and infinite, thus confounding together the most contradictory conceptions; for the moment a personality becomes defined and distinct, it ceases to be possible to conceive it as infinite.

------

[1] They may be rare, but occultism knows and the world feels the malice of such unhappy beings.—*Trans*.

It is through Ignorance that men have insisted on
constraining each other now to submit to a Faith
without Reason, now to lean upon Reason without
Faith, mutually persecuting each other, to recoil in
turn to the two poles of Folly.

It is through Ignorance of the Laws of Nature
that men have believed in the sun being arrested in
its course, in asses speaking, in the jaw bones of an
ass transforming themselves into fountains, and in a
whole world of absurdities and chimeras.

It is Ignorance that makes Trimalchio burst at
table, and St. Anthony go mad in the desert, man
ever craving to plunge into vices or scale the heights
to virtues disproportioned to his being.

It is through Ignorance that Tiberius, at Capri, in-
flicted on himself sensual gratifications more horrible
than tortures, and felt himself die a thousand times
daily in the disgust of his power, and the agony of
his pleasures.

The Ignorant have poisoned Socrates, crucified
Jesus Christ, tortured the martyrs, burnt the heretics,
massacred the priests, have overthrown and re-erected
alternately the most monstrous idols, have preached,
some tyranny, others license, have denied, some all
authority, others liberty, and all have ignored Reason,
Truth and Justice.

It is through Ignorance that a man is proud since
he then fancies to make himself honoured by rendering himself ridiculous and contemptible.

It is through Ignorance that a man is avaricious
since he thus makes *himself* the slave of what is made

to serve *us*. It is through Ignorance that a man becomes a debauchee, since he thus makes a *deadly* abuse of what should relate to and propagate *Life*.

Through Ignorance men mutually hate in lieu of loving, isolate themselves instead of helping one the other, separate instead of associating, corrupt instead of improving each other, destroy in place of preserving and weaken themselves in egoism in lieu of strengthening themselves in universal charity.

Man naturally seeks that which he believes to be good, and if he almost always deceives himself, foolishly and cruelly, it is that he does not *know*. The Despots of the old world did not know that the abuse of Power involves the fall of Power, and that in digging the earth to hide their victims they were digging their own graves. The Revolutionists of all times have not known that anarchy being the conflict of Lusts and the fatal reign of Violence, substitutes might for right, and paves the way ever for the rule of the most audaciously criminal.

The Inquisitors did not know that in the name of the Church they were burning Jesus Christ, that in the name of the Holy Office they were burning the Gospel, and that the ashes of their *auto-da-fés* would brand indelibly on their foreheads the mark of Cain.

Voltaire, in preaching God and Liberty, did not know that in the narrow minds of the vulgar Liberty destroyed God; he did not know that in the dark foundations of symbols hides a light sublime; that the Bible is a Babel on the summit of which rests the Holy Ark; and he never thought he was preparing

the materials for the impious farces of Chaumette
and the paradoxes of Proudhon.

Rousseau did not know that amongst the bastard
children of his proud and fretful genius he would
have one day to reckon Robespierre and Marat.

Paschal but ill knew mathematics since he believed
in the Jansenists. When the exactitude of proportions and equilibrium demonstrated to him justness
everywhere in the Universe, how could this incon-
sistent geometer suppose injustice in God ?

If the Monks of the Middle Ages had known Phys-
iology and Medicine, they would have known that
solitude drives men mad, that night-watches inflame
the blood, that fasts deprive the brain of blood, and
compulsory celibacy provokes unnatural frenzies.[1]

If Bossuet and Newton had known the Kabala,
they would not have explained the Apocalypse without understanding it.

If Napoleon III had known mathematics he would
not have attacked Prussia.

No man knowingly deceives himself, and he who
flies from Truth does not know what Truth is.

Each one yields to what attracts him most strong-
ly, and the predominance of attraction depends on
knowledge.

---

[1] Nothing of the kind, when the Spirit is naturally
stronger than and has mastered Flesh at the start.
Besides, there is the will ! But with the Spirit half
slumbering and the Will but half awake, it is folly to
try it at all.—E. O.

To live is to suffer ; to know *how* to live is to be happy.

To love is to obey ; to know *how* to love is to rule.

To speak is to make a noise; to know *how* to speak is to make melody.

To seek is to torment oneself ; to know *how* to seek is to find.

To use is often to abuse ; to know *how* to use is to enjoy.

To practise magic is to be a quack ; to *know* magic is to be a sage.

To believe without knowing is to be a fool ; to know without believing is to be a mad man ; true knowledge brings with it faith.[1]

The man who knows has no longer cause to doubt ; when the Spirit no longer doubts, the will ceases to hesitate and the man attains to what he wills.

To this question " Why has God created us ? " Catholicism replies, " To love, know, and serve him and thus merit eternal Life ".

Let us say the same thing in simpler words. We are in the world to love ; when we love, we love God, *because God only manifests himself to us in Nature, and in Man.*

We are in the world to learn, that is to say to *know*; to learn everything is to know God more and more. The true Theology is the Universal Science.

---

[1] A great Paradox, but also a great truth, when rightly understood.—E. O.

We are in the world to serve **Humanity, which** is
serving God, [1] by consecrating to it our **free** activity.
Thus shall we march on in the Eternal Progress.

No one *earns* Eternal Life by his merits; this
imposes *itself* on us, and if we do not know how to
enjoy it we still have to accept it.

Knowledge is the first power of the intelligent
Universe. God is the master of infinite knowledge.
He who knows is naturally the master of him who
knows not. It is necessary to know, in order to be.
He who does not know how to be rich, *is* not rich ;
he who does not know how to be good, *is* not good,
Knowledge is proportional to being, and in philosophy,
as Kant remarked, being is identical with knowing.

---

[1] What a ridiculous supernumerary, such a God
before the Jury of Sense and Logic. Nevertheless
some of the most sensible men loathe the idea of
parting with this fiction.—E. O.

Amongst our Fiji fellow subjects, the ships,
the judges, the governors and other manifestations of our good Queen are received with
respect and love ; in her name justice is done
between man and man, her name protects all
from the assaults of foreign nations ; she is only
known to them by pictures (more or less fancy
portraits) or by the effects accomplished by and in
her name, and these Fijians can only serve her by
good citizenship, dealing fairly and uprightly with
their fellow subjects. Truly a ridiculous supernumerary is the actual Queen Victoria ! and yet some of
the most sensible Fijians would loathe to part with
this fiction, nay—would think a man overhasty who
denounced her as a myth.—*Trans.*

Knowledge alone confers a right of property. We interdict those who do not know how to use their wealth. Abuse springs from an ignorance, more or less voluntary, of how to use. He who knows how to acquire and preserve, has the right to use ; no one has the right to abuse.

As a guarantee of the rights of the individual, property is sacred, for it is the expression of the right to labour and constitutes the power to give and to lend which is the dignity of man ; but it is limited by social duty, *each one owing himself to all, and all to each*, in the degrees prescribed by Order, Justice and Law.

To ignore this is to become liable to accept as a Truth Proudhon's paradox, " *La propriété c'est le vol.*" Ignorance is the mother of all Revolutions, because she is the cause of all injustice.

When a man *knows*, he is master of all who do *not* know ; Study is the ladder of merit and of power. First amongst necessary studies *is the study of one-self*; then comes the study of the exact sciences,[1] then of Nature, then of History. It is from these preparatory studies that are to be gathered the elements of Philosophy which must be perfected by the Science of Religions.

A Mage could not be ignorant : magic signifies majority, and majority signifies emancipation by knowledge.

---

[1] *i.e., Occult* Sciences.—E. O.

The Latin word *magister*, which means master, is derived, as well as the word magistrate, from the words Magic and Mage.

Magis signifies more, *major*, more great—in a word magic implies superiority.

It is for this reason that the Christian legend of the Epiphany confounds the Magi (or Mages) with the kings and brings them to the manger of the Saviour of men, guided by the mysterious star of Solomon.[1]

Jesus in his cradle is saluted Prince of the Magi, and they offer him incense of Saba, gold of Ophir and myrrh of Memphis. Because he comes to consecrate anew the fire of Zoroaster, to renovate the symbolic treasures of Hiram, and bind up once more the mutilated form of Osiris with the fillets of Hermes.

The Magi, guided by the star of Sabaism, came to honour the infancy of the Christian initiation, then to elude the violence of Herod they returned homewards by another road. What is that road ? It is that of occultism. The powers of this world ignore it, but it is known to the initiated Johannites, Adoniramites, Illuminati and Rosicrucians.[2]

---

[1] In one of the secret books of Merop—a book antedating Christianity, three Magi are shown as seeking the lost wisdom of Zoroaster in order to save mankind from *maya*,—ignorance. A star appears, a six-pointed star, and leads them to the cave where Zarathushtra's Book of Wisdom is buried.—E. O.

[2] And other more important sects, associations and fraternities, whose names, even, have never been divulged to the world.—*Trans.*

We must *know*, to *will* with reason. When we
will with reason, it is our right and duty to dare,
but when we are not sheltered from perverse and
senseless attacks, we must keep silence as to what
we dare.

We may, but ought not, always to assert what we
know ; we ought to be free and avow what we
believe, but the Christ did not advise this when he
said, " Cast not your pearls before swine, lest they
turn again and rend you."

Occult science has, therefore, a reason for its
secrecy, and that reason is declared, and as it were
sanctioned, by an authority at once human and
divine.

Did Jesus himself follow his own precept ? The
pearls of his doctrine, were they not trampled under
foot by the obscene brutes who devoured him, and
even still devour him ? We shall not answer that
question, but at the risk of our repose, of our
reputation, and even if needs be our life, we have
ever striven, still strive and shall strive to the end,
to rescue from the swine's trough the pearls of the
Holy Gospel.

The Occult sciences are no more the authorised
sciences than is the religion of the initiated that of
the common believer.

They move onwards ever, guessing what is not
yet defined. They brave not the anathema, but move
on heeding it not, for no anathema can reach them.

It is certain that there exist in nature and in man
forces which as yet escape the control of the most

4

learned authorities. Magnetism is still a problem
that the Academicians will not investigate. The
Kabala is unknown to Rabbis of the second Talmud ;
the name, even, of magic raises a smile on the faces
of our professors of Physics, and it is well understood
that a man's mind must be deranged who in these
days occupies himself with the Hermetic Philosophy.

Trismegistus, Orpheus, Pythagoras, Apollonius,
Porphyry, Paracelsus, Trithemus, Pomponavius,
Vaneni, Giordano Bruno and so many others, were
they all mad ?

Count Joseph de Maistre, that fiery Ultramontane,
did not believe it ; he who recognised the necessity
of a new manifestation turned his eyes, against his
will, towards the sanctuaries of Occultism.

*All Religions and all Sciences connect themselves
with one single science, always hidden from the
common herd, and transmitted from age to age, from
initiate to initiate, beneath the veil of fables and
symbols.* It preserves for a world yet to come the
secrets of a world that has passed away. The
Gymnosophists contemplated it on the banks of the
Ganges ; Zoroaster and Hermes preserved it in the
East ; Moses transmitted it to the Hebrews ; Orpheus
revealed its mysteries to Greece ; Pythagoras and
Plato almost guessed it. It was called the Priestly
or Royal Science, because it raised the initiated to
the ranks of Kings and Pontiffs ; it is portrayed in
the Bible by the mysterious personage Melchisedec,
the peaceful king and eternal priest, who has neither
father nor mother nor genealogy. He stands by

himself like Truth. Christian initiates have said
that Christ was the same personage as this Melchisedec, and Jesus himself seems to have adopted this
allegory when he says that he existed before Abraham,
who hailed him rejoicing to see his light. This
science of the Priests and Kings was on this account
called the Holy Kingdom, the Kingdom of Heaven,
the Kingdom of God. All cannot reach it; it is
accessible only to the élite of intelligences, and it is
on this account that, according to the Gospels, few
are chosen. This science conceals itself because it is
persecuted,[1] Zoroaster was burnt,[2] Osiris cut in
pieces, Orpheus torn in fragments by the Bacchantes,
Phythagoras assassinated, Socrates, Plato's Master,
poisoned, the great prophets put to death in diverse
ways, Jesus crucified, his apostles doomed to martyrdom; but the doctrine never dies, and though it
disappears it must ever return. It is on this account
that the Legends, more true than History *when we
know how to interpret them,* tell us that Enoch and
Elias are living in Heaven, and will redescend to
earth. It is on this account that Jesus was raised
from the dead, and that St. John was not to
die. These forms of speech are of the essence of

---

[1] By human ignorance and folly.—E. O.

[2] I don't know that E. L. has any valid authority
for this statement. It is usually stated that he died
at a good old age, about 313 B.C., though some
authorities speak of his being murdered a year later
in the persecution of Arjasp.—*Trans.*

Occultism. They show and yet conceal the Truth.
What the initiate says is true, but what the
profane understand is a falsehood made for them.
*Truth is like Liberty and Virtue; she yields not
herself, she must be sought and conquered.*
It is said that at the death of the Christ the Veil of
the Temple was rent. This means that occult science
was no longer there; she still lived, but at the foot of
the cross of the Master who had passed away. An
apostle, he who is represented as always young,
became the second son of Mary, and meditated a
book of which his Gospel is but a reflection, and
which was fated never to be understood by the orthodox Church of the uninitiated. The Apocalypse of
St. John is a new veil denser than that of Moses, but
enriched with broideries, grand, splendid, hung, to
the despair of the usurpers of Priesthood and
Kingship, before the sanctuary of the Eternal
Truth.

The Apocalypse is entirely unintelligible for the
uninitiated, for it is a book of the Kabala.

We have explained in our former works what the
Kabala is, and we have indicated for intelligent
readers the key of the secrets contained in that sublime
volume.

The author of the Apocalypse does not write for
simple believers, but for those who *know*, and he often
repeats, "Here is the science, let him who has the
knowledge calculate and find the number." His
Philosophy is that of the Word, that is to say of the
Reason which speaks.

Jesus, like all great Hierophants, had a public and
a secret doctrine.[1] His public doctrine differed only
in its morality from Judaism. He preached to all
universal philanthropy, and upheld the Law of Moses
while combating the brutalising influence of a hypocritical and overweening priesthood. But his secret

[1] But he preached it a century before his birth.—
E. O.

I may explain that some of the most eminent
occultists hold the Gospel Christ to be an ideal, based
upon a Jesus who lived a considerable time before
anno Domini. This Jesus, Jeshu Ben Panthera,
lived from about 120 to 70 B.C., was a pupil of
Rabbi Joachim Ben Perachia, his grand uncle, with
whom, during the persecution of the Jews by Alexander Jannæus, he fled to Alexandria, and was
initiated into the Egyptian mysteries, or magic. On
his return to Palestine this Jeshu was charged with,
and convicted of, heresy and sorcery (he was unques-
tionably an adept) and hung on *the tree of infamy*
(the Roman Cross) outside the city of Lud or Lydda.
This man was a historical character, and his life and
death are indubitably established. Why they look
upon the Gospel Christ as an ideal, based upon the
Jesus, is that there is no contemporaneous or nearly
contemporaneous record by reliable historians of the
Gospel Christ. The only passage in Josephus
referring to Jesus Christ is now admitted on all sides
to be a pure forgery. Clearly Josephus never men-
tioned Christ, whereas had the gospel narratives been
correct he must have done so. Again, " Philo
Judæus, the most learned of the historians, contemporaneous to the Jesus of the Gospels, a man whose
birth anteceded and whose death succeeded the birth
and death of Jesus, respectively by ten or fifteen

doctrine he only revealed to his beloved apostle who
was to revive it after his death.   This doctrine was

---

years ; who visited Jerusalem from Alexandria several
times during his long career, and must have been at
Jerusalem shortly after the crucifixion ; who, in
describing the various religious sects, societies and
corporations of Palestine, takes the greatest care to
omit none, noticing even the most insignificant, never
apparently heard and (certainly never mentions) anything about Christ, the crucifixion or any other of
the facts commemorated in the Gospels."   Further,
they ask if Christ really lived at the time alleged
how is it that absolutely no reference to him is found
in the Mishna.   " The Mishna was founded by Hillel
4o B.C., and edited and amplified (till about the beginning of the third century of our era) at Tiberias by
the sea of Galilee, the very focus of the doings of the
Biblical apostles and Christ's miracles.   The Mishna
contains an unbroken record of all the Heresiarchs
and rebels against the authority of the Jewish
Sanhedrin, is in short a diary of the doings of the
synagogue and a history of the Pharisees, those same
men who are accused of having put Jesus to death."
How is it possible, it is asked, that if the gospel
narratives were true, and the events therein recorded
really occurred at the time alleged, no reference
whatsoever to these decidedly important (even though
the Rabbis believed Jesus to be an impostor) trans-
actions is to be found in this very elaborate chronicle,
whose special object it was to record all heresies,
schisms and matters generally affecting the orthodox
Jewish religion ?

It will now be understood what E. O. means when
he says Jesus preached a hundred years before his
birth.—*Trans.*

not new. A great Jew, an initiate, Ezekiel, had sketched it out before St. John. God in Humanity and in Nature, the Universal Church of the just, the progressive enfranchisement of mankind, the assumption of the Woman,[1] to be loved as Virgin, adored as Mother, the destruction of the despotism of Priests

---

[1] While the vulgar, the masses, were convinced of the influence of the Two Lights (*Mar-oth*, lights, Sun and Moon, from *Mairo* to shine ; *Maria*—the Lord) of Heaven upon the living beings on earth, the initiates knew what these lights were. Osiris and Isis were named Apollo and Diana in the West, and when the Christian Bishops began their work of fitting in and accommodating things to their newly conceived doctrine, they rejected Apollo and Diana, Balder and Freia, and invented Christus and Maria. I. A. H. according to the Kabalists is, I [father] and A. H. [mother] composed of I the male and H the female. Jah is Adam, Evah is Eve, together the doubleman (male and female created he them) of Christ, of Genesis and the Kabala.

" Through a Virgin, the Eva (h), came the death ; it was *necessary* through a *Virgin* but more *from* a Virgin that the LIFE should appear," says the wily Cyril. *Hiersol.* XII, VI.

The Alchemists call *akasa* the Virgin. All lite passes through *akasa* into earth.

Hence Christ's coming on earth through Mary (*Mar*) the Virgin.

" Screaming *Evoe Bakke* (Bacchus), thou alone art worthy of the Virgin."—*Æneid VII*, 389.

It is on the soil of Asia sprung from the teachings of Oriental *initiates* that two conceptions were

and Kings, the reign of Truth and Justice, the union
of Science and Faith, the final annihilation of the
three hideous phantoms, the Devil, Death and Hell,
whom St. John flings down and buries for ever in a
lake of fire and brimstone, the definite establishment
upon earth of the New Jerusalem, a city which no
longer needs temples as it is itself a temple, where no
priests or kings are seen because all the inhabitants
are Priests and Kings, an ideal but realisable city

---

evolved that have chiefly determined the Religious
convictions of the Christians :

(1) The doctrine of ONE EXISTENCE, Parabrahm,
our one Life, which is this primal and sole principle
of the universe.

(2) That of LIGHT (*akasa* with its seven principles)
which became the Logos of Christians ; for " sound "
emanates from *akasa*.

PRIMAL LIFE manifests itself by its intelligence,
Logos or wisdom, seventh principle, considered as the
primal *male* principle. In this stage of the conception, the wisdom is identical with spirit or Purusha,
with the Hindu the primal divine male. The Old
Testament uses the wisdom, spirit and word as
synonymous expressions.

The two existences or lights were called, ages
B.C., FATHER and SON.

Sabda, " sound " or " word," is constantly mention-
ed in our Mimānsa philosophy. Compare with the
Greek *Logos*, the " eternity of sound " a dogma of
Mimānsa, relating with us to the eternal verities of
the occult truth. With the non-initiated Hindus,
the eternity of *Sabda* shows the eternity of the
Vedas.—E. O.

where Liberty, Equality and Fraternity might reign,
a city of the elect, of the just, where the vile
multitude will never enter, archetype of human
civilisation, Land promised to all but accessible only
to the elect, not of privilege but by labour, not by
the caprice of an idol but by the justice of God.

Such is the ideal of knowledge.[1]

Paradox V.—REASON IS GOD

THIS should be placed first. It is before everything :
it is self-existent, it exists even for those who do not
know it, as the Sun for the Blind, but to see it, feel
it, understand it, this is the triumph of the understanding in man ; it is the definite result of all the
travail of thought and all the aspirations of Faith.

In the principle is Reason, and Reason is in God,
and God is Reason.[2] All is made by it, and without

---

[1] The " Eternal Wisdom " *lia ckakama lia kadama*
of the Hebrew Kabala unites with the Soul of the
Messias : " *Sair anpin* in truth is the *Soul* of the
Messias joined with the eternal *Logos.*"—*Kabala
III*, 241 Jezira.—E. O.

[2] Our version reads : " In the beginning was the
Word," etc., but neither reading adequately conveys
the occult sense of the passage. The *arche* is the
primordial evolute, which the ONE unconsciously
emanates, the beginning of all things. The *logos* is
the Law of Evolution, the reason of all things, itself
the cause of their complex inter-relations, the Word,

it is nothing made. It is the true light that enlightens us from our birth : it shines even in the darkness, but the darkness does not close it in.

These words are the oracle of Reason itself, and they occur, as all know, at the commencement of the Gospel of St. John.

Without this Reason nothing exists ; everything has its reason for existing, even unreason,[1] which serves as a background to reason as the shadow does to the light.

---

the Force or Energy that everywhere and in all time, regulates, and *is*, at the same time, the mainspring of the universe.—*Trans.*

[1] This is an instance of Eliphas Levi's persistent habit of at one time using words in their occult senses, and at another, perhaps in the same sentence, in their popular senses, so as to lead the unwary to the conclusion that he is using them throughout in these latter. Of course there is no *alogos, no* such thing as " *déraison*," if *raison* is to be construed in its occult sense. All through his writings he grasps at any apparently neat antithesis, no matter how false it may be, or how much he thereby risks misleading the most worthy student as to his real meaning. Unreason acting as a background to show up reason is nonsense, if reason be taken in its occult sense in which he has been using it in the previous lines, viz., of the force or law or impulse or design, or all put together, without which nothing can have come into being, and which accounts for all that exists, because Unreason has no occult sense, and in its popular sense is as much an evolute of the *logos*, as is Reason, in the ordinary signification of the word ; but E. L.

The reasonable believer is he who believes in a reason greater than knowledge ; for the reason, or to speak more correctly the reasoning of each one, is not absolute wisdom.

When I reason ill, I become unreasonable [1] ; it is not then reason that I should distrust, but my own judgment.

I should turn then willingly to those who know more than I do, but even then I must have reason to believe in their superiority.

To conjecture, at random, what one does not know, and then believe blindly in one's own conjectures, or in those of others, who know no more than ourselves, is to behave like madmen. When we are told that God demands the sacrifice of our reason,

---

could not resist the jingle of Reason and Unreason, and so without warning in the middle of the sentence he uses " Reason," for the first time in the discourse, in its restricted exoteric meaning. Moreover having laid down some law or truth in words bearing, and intended by him to bear, some broad occult sense, he constantly goes on to argue on or *play* with these in their restricted commonplace significations, introducing thus a confusion of ideas, utterly bewildering to the reader, even if the writer did not, as I suspect, frequently himself lose touch with the Higher Doctrine. If these weaknesses of our author be kept in mind, many apparent difficulties in all his works will disappear.—*Trans.*

[1] The original is, *Quand je raisonne mal, je n'ai point raison,* a play on words which can only be approximated in English as above.

this is to make God, the ideal or despotic idol, of folly.

Reason gives conviction, but rash belief produces only infatuation.

It is quite reasonable to believe in things that one neither sees, touches, nor measures, because manifestly the infinite exists, and one can say not only I believe, but *I know* that an infinity of things exist which are beyond my reach.

Knowledge being indefinitely progressive, I can believe that I shall one day know that of which I am now ignorant. I have no doubts in regard to what I know thoroughly; I may doubt my knowledge if I know imperfectly, but I cannot have doubts as to a thing of which I know nothing, since it is impossible for me to formulate them.

He who says there is no God, without having defined God in a complete and absolute manner, simply talks nonsense. I wait for his definition, and when he has set this forth after his own fashion, I am certain, beforehand, of being able to say to him, " I agree with you, there *is* no *such* God "; but that God is certainly not my God. If he says to me : " Define your God," I should reply, " I will take good care to do nothing of the kind, for a God defined is a God dethroned.[1] Every positive definition is deniable, the Infinite is the undefined. " I believe only in matter,"

---

[1] The original play upon the words, "*un Dieu défini est un Dieu fini*" cannot be exactly reproduced in English.—*Trans*.

another will tell me, but what *is* matter? In surgery they give that name to excretions, and one might say in philosophy, somewhat paradoxically, that matter is the excretion of thought. The materialists fully deserve to be paid off with this somewhat coarse and Carnivallic definition, they who declare thought the excretion of the material brain, without realising that this admirable and passive instrument of the workings of the human soul is the masterpiece of a thought, which is not ours.

If I could define God, in a certain and positive manner, I should cease to *believe* in God, I should *know* what he is, but not being able to *know* this, I simply *believe* that he exists, *because it is impossible for me not to conceive a directive thought, in this eternally living substance that peoples infinite space.*[1]

---

[1] Within that Substance, within every atom of it, but not outside of it. There is no extra-cosmic Deity. *All* matter is God, and God is Matter, or there is no God.—E. O.

This seems to me begging the question. Has any one been outside the Cosmos to look? E. O. may reply Cosmos is infinite, there can be nothing *outside* what is infinite, forgetting, it seems to me, that what may be infinite to all conditioned in it, may yet leave room for a beyond to the Unconditioned. He admits a fourth dimension of space, and asserts further on, as will be seen, and as I believe with good reason, that there are yet fifth, sixth and seventh dimensions of space to be discovered, yet he desires to insist that the conceptions of intelligences (I give him in the planetary spirits and all) conditioned in

If believers in exclusive Religions tell me that God
has revealed himself and that he has spoken, I reply
I do not *believe* it, I *know* it.   I know that God
reveals himself to the human heart in the beauties of
Nature; I know that he has spoken by the voices of
all the wise and in the hearts of all the just.   I read
his words, in the hymns of Cleanthus and Orpheus, as
in the Psalms of David; I admire the grand pages
of the Vedas and of the Koran, and find the legend
of Krishna as touching as a gospel, but I wax wroth
against Jupiter torturing Prometheus and serving as
a pretext for the death of Socrates.   I shudder when

---

the Cosmos, which *we* can only think of as infinite,
are absolute; whereas I submit, that they are
necessarily relative, and that the fact that the highest
intelligences conditioned in the universe *believe* it to
be infinite and can trace in it nothing but laws, by
no means *proves* that to a still higher and unconditioned
intelligence there may not be something outside that
infinity, and in that something the intelligence whose
will the discoverable Laws represent.   Nay, further, I
submit that intelligence *may* be inside and pervading
the Cosmos, and yet be incognisable for its own good
reasons by all its emanated intelligences.   To me therefore the assertion that either " God is matter " (in the
sense of unconscious unintelligent substance) " or
there is no God," appears equally rash and unphilo-
sophical.   I fully understand the refusal to acknow-
ledge or believe in that, of which no knowledge exists,
and of which no evidence can be obtained, but this
seems to me wholly different from denying its existence, which involves the assumption of omniscience.
—*Trans.*

I hear the Christ reproaching, in his last dying sobs,
Jehovah for having abandoned him, and I veil my
face when Alexander VI professes to represent Jesus
Christ. The executioners and tormentors of the
human conscience are as odious to me under the
priestly reign of Pius VI as under that of Nero. The
*true Christian Religion is humanity, superhuman in
the strength of forgiveness, and the sacrifice of self
for others.*

The Gods to whom are sacrificed men are Demons.
Reason should for ever thrust away the worship of
these Demons, and the idol of the Devil, which has
become ridiculous by it, is monstrosity. *Those who
believe in the Devil, worship the Devil, for they
worship his Creator and . . . accomplice.* We have
already said, *The God of the Devil, who reproves the
Devil and yet still allows him to work on for our
destruction is a horrible fiction of human wickedness
and cowardice;* a God of the Devil turned round
would become a Devil of a God. Thus speaks
reason, but superstition would still impose silence,
and that is why many people, excusably enough,
leave, while pitying them, to the superstitious their
God and their Devil, and themselves believe thenceforth in nothing.

But even superstition has its *raison d'être* in the
infinities of the human intellect. The Priesthood has
succeeded in converting it into a force, by subjecting
it to blind obedience. Take away superstition from
souls, narrow but ardent, and you convert them into
fanatics of impiety. One must e'en restrain fools

through their folly[1], since they are not *willing* to be wise.

We teach morality to children by telling them stories, and the nurses take good care not to disabuse their minds when they are frightened at Bogy. It is true that certain realistic mothers threaten their children with the wolf or the policeman, but neither wolf nor policeman can be everywhere, and the child, convinced of their absence, will laugh at the threat, whereas Bogy, who is never seen anywhere, is believed, like the Devil, to be present everywhere, and. the child is all the more impelled to believe in it because it is a fiction, a poetic delusion, a story—in one word something that takes hold on the imagination, and the imagination, powerful in men, is supreme in children.

Bogy is the children's Devil, just as the Devil of the Middle Ages was the Bogy of men.

Moreover there is no fiction which does not serve as a veil or mask for some reality. Bogy exists, and the poor child will soon know him in the guise of a frowning pedant with harsh voice and more or less justly applied cane.

Then they will tell him about God and the Devil in such terms that he might easily mistake one for the other. Will he then continue satisfied with the

---

[1] And I must say he puts this precept into practice admirably; while laughing at the fools with one corner of the mouth, he strengthens their folly with the other.—E. O.

conclusion of the drama of Punch? Punch made him
laugh, the Devil wanted to make him cry; would
he not wish that in the end, Punch, so often carried
off by the Devil, should in his turn carry off the
Devil? This would be a question of temperament
and audacity.

Ancient Hierophants have always held that it
would be the greatest crime to admit the multitude to
the initiations because it would be to let loose the
wolves, open the paddock of the fallow deer, and
plunge all men in war one with the other under the
pretext of equality.

Jesus Christ enjoined upon his disciples not to cast
their pearls before swine. The Freemasons to this day
swear to preserve to the death the secrets which they
no longer possess. Equality amongst men can only
exist by Hierarchical grades; it can never be absolute, because Nature disallows it. There must be
great and little, so that men may mutually assist, and
have need of, each other.

Nothing is more difficult for the common run of
men than to live according to reason, and do good
for the sake of good. Their motive is almost always
desire or fear, and they are to be led by hope or
dread. They require, moreover, restraint to prevent
their falling into inertia or disorder. They march
better when in regiments and loaded; the monk and
the soldier rejoice under an iron discipline; it is by
austerities and silence that the inconstancy of woman
disappears. One man lives courageously the life of a
Trappist who would be a robber, did he not long for

5

Heaven and fear Hell. Is he the better for this?
Perhaps not, but certainly it is less dangerous for
Society.

It is all very fine to tell the truth to men, but they
will not understand it unless they have already
themselves sought for and almost found it. The
world of Tiberius wanted expiations and austerities.
The age of the Platonists and Stoics, of Seneca and
Epictetus, was bound to embrace the Christian
Morality. Virgil seems to sing near to the manger
of the Man-God, and the Sibylline books promised
the Christ to earth!

Luther was not carried by his *own* impulse against
Rome; he was lifted and pushed forward by a
current that swept over all Europe. Voltaire did
not make the eighteenth century, it was the
eighteenth century which made Voltaire. The reign
of Madame de Maintenon and the scandals of
Jansenism had disgusted and wearied France to the
last degree; the funereal orisons of Bossuet seemed
to have interred the Christian Monarchy, and there
followed Cardinals like Bernel and like Dubois.
Voltaire scoffed at everything and made people
laugh. Rousseau, however, professed that there
was something in it, and people admired while persecuting him, because in their hearts the world was
somewhat of his way of thinking. The revolutionists
out-Rousseau'd Rousseau, and the good sense of the
country sided with Chateaubriand, though all the
while applauding the Voltairian rogueries of
Béranger : it is progress that brings great men to the

front, and the world wrongly credits them with the movement which has made them conspicuous.

The French Revolution presented a strange and ridiculous spectacle to the world, when it inaugurated the worship of Reason, personified by an opera dancer. One might have fancied that the nation was making fun of itself, and desired to avow to other nations that the reason of the French is almost always folly.

Then it was that Robespierre, to dethrone this indecent Reason, invented his Supreme Being, but public opinion would not ratify the change; it remembered God and realised that the Revolution was shifting its ground. Bonaparte, who followed, understood that Religion was not dead, but Religion for him could only be Catholic, in other words, authoritative; he re-opened the Churches, and tried to lay his hand on the Pope, but the Pope slipped from him with the world.

It is that the reason of Religion is superior to the reason of Politics, because it is only in Religion that right takes the lead of might. For a right to be inviolable it must be proclaimed as Divine. Right and Duty are above man, God preserves the one, in imposing the other on him; God is the Supreme Reason.

A body cannot live without a head, and the head of the social body is God. A body changes but does not die, if its head be immortal. God is the Truth and Justice that never change; it is for this cause that the state should give way to religious reasons. The

Church is the prototype of the Fatherland; it is the Universal Fatherland, and the unity of the Christian world [1] is something greater than the unity of Germany or Italy.

Moral force is superior to physical force, and spiritual power gets the upper hand of temporal power. If St. Peter had never drawn his sword, Jesus would never have said to him, " When thou shalt be old, thou shalt stretch forth thy hands, and another shall gird thee, and carry thee whither thou wouldest not." The King of Italy has taken Rome from the Holy Father, because St. Peter took by force the ear of Malchus. Malchus or Male signifies, in Hebrew, the king. Be it as it may, the capital of the Christian world ought not to belong exclusively to Italy. The supreme representative of Divine Humanity ought to be a priest to bless and a king to pardon. That is what reason tells us, and if the Pope *believes* that a father of a family ought to be infallible for his children, that the head of religion ought to have no dealings with irreligion; that liberty of conscience ought not to be permitted; if he *believes* himself obliged to turn society upside down; if he protests, in a word, against each and everything that appears to him contrary to dogma, why, setting aside the justice of the question, the Pope is a thousand times right! [2]

---

[1] But when or where has such Unity ever existed? —*Trans.*

[2] It is scarcely necessary to tell most readers that all this is elaborate chaff. Still our author's

Next to the passions, the greatest enemies of human reason are the prejudices. We do not examine *how* things are; we simply will that they should be in such and such a way. We refuse to change our opinion, because this humiliates our pride, as if man was born infallible, and should not day by day instruct and perfect himself. " When I was a child," said St. Paul, " I spake as a child, I understood as a child, I thought as a child : but when I became a man, I put away childish things." The apostle here proclaims the law of progress and even applies it to the Church, but this is what the theologians obstinately refuse to understand.

We must distrust devout prejudices as much as impious prejudices. True piety is essentially independent, but she submits herself reasonably to customs and laws, when she cannot hope, and even often when she does hope, to change them.

Jesus would not that they should pluck up the tares which were mixed with the wheat, for fear lest at the same time they should uproot the good grain ; but that they should wait for the harvest, and then separate the wheat from the evil weeds. There are epochs of summing up and synthesis, in which criticism ought to distinguish the true from the false. We are at one of such epochs in which prejudices ought

persistent habit of saying, apparently seriously, what he does not believe and what he does not mean any one but " *les fous* " to believe, is likely too often to become seriously misleading to this latter large and respectable class.—*Trans.*

no longer to be tenderly handled. Nevertheless, we must not be harsh with the people who hold them. Let us show, softly and patiently, the truth, and the falsehoods will fall of their own accord.[1]

Prejudices are the bad habits of the mind; they spring from education, from ignorance or intellectual sloth, from interests of position, reputation or fortune. We readily believe in the truth of what pleases us and still more readily in what flatters us; the best feelings, even when exaggerated, become sources of prejudice; the love of family produces pride and the intolerance of caste; the love of country gives place to national arrogance; people think that they should be French, or English, rather than that they should be *men* : religious enthusiasm leads on to many other excesses. Succeeding ages despise, condemn and execrate each other; the Christians are dogs for the followers of Muhammad, the Jews are obscene beings for the Christian, the Protestants are Heretics, the Catholics are Papists . . . where are the reasonable men ?

Reason is like Truth ; she shocks when seen naked.

To be too much in the right is to be in the wrong. Reason should persuade and not impose herself. She has little power over children, and almost always displeases women.

---

[1] This is true, but only half the Truth. *Per contra* remember that the longer you let the weeds stand, the wider will their seeds be disseminated, and the larger and stubborner the growth you will have to deal with.—*Trans*.

She is a power, but it is an occult power; she should govern without showing her hand.[1]

It requires a very powerful and firm mind to devote oneself without danger to the occult sciences, and above all to the experiences which confirm their theories; magnetism, divination and spiritualism still people the madhouses, and the Hermetic Philosophy may add further victims. The most celebrated proficients in these sciences have had their moments of aberration. Pythagoras remembered to have been Euphorbius. Apollonius of Tyana caused an old beggar to be stoned to stay the Plague. Paracelsus believed that he had a familiar spirit hidden in the pommel of his long sword.[2] Cardan allowed himself to die of hunger to justify astrology. Duchenteau, who reconstructed and completed the magic calendar of Tycho-Brahe, also died miserably in attempting an extravagant experiment. Cagliostro compromised himself with a set of rogues, in the matter of the Queen's necklace, and went away to die in the dungeons of Rome. The interior of the ark is not to be looked at with impunity, and those who will touch it run the risk of being struck like Moza by lightning.

---

[1] He seems to draw but a feeble line between "the Occult" and "the Jesuitical".—E.O.

Doubtless because he himself, like many other occultists, was avowedly somewhat Jesuitical in his dealings with non-initiates.—*Trans.*

[2] Eliphas, as usual, is here poking fun at his *Public*. He is perfectly aware that all these pretended traits of madness have an occult signification.—*Trans.*

*I do not speak of the fear, the envy, the hate of the
vulgar which everywhere pursue the Initiate, who
does not know how to conceal his knowledge. True
sages escape from this danger.*[1] The Abbé Trithemus
lived and died peacefully while Agrippa, his
imprudent disciple, closed prematurely in a hospital
a life of disquietude and torment. Agrippa, before
his death, blasphemed against the Science, as Brutus
at Philippi had blasphemed against Virtue, but
despite the despair of Brutus, Virtue is more than an
empty name, and despite the discouragement of
Agrippa, Science[2] is a Truth.

At the present day, occult sciences are scarcely
studied except by presumptuous ignoramuses or eccentric savants ; women furnish their necessary ground, in
hysterical crises and doubtful somnambulism. People
want above all things prodigies ; to cog the dice of
Fortune, to shuffle the cards of Fate, to have philtres
and amulets, to bewitch their enemies, to put jealous
husbands to sleep, to discover the universal panacea
of all the vices, not to reform them, but to preserve
them from the two great diseases that kill them—
deception and lassitude—countenance such schemes,
and one is sure to travel quickly on the high road of
folly. If the hasty Achilles of Homer had been
wholly invulnerable, he would only have been a

---

[1] I am glad he admits the principle.—E. O.
The principle " *de dissimuler* " ? I fear it is a
principle *all* are only *too* ready to admit.—*Trans.*
[2] He means here of course *Occult* Science.—*Trans.*

cowardly assassin, and the man who was sure of always gaining at play would soon ruin every one, and ought to be branded as a swindler. *He who by a single act of his Will could entail on others sickness or death, would be a public pest, of whom Society ought to rid itself;* to win love, save by natural means, is to commit a sort of violation; *to evoke shades is to call down upon oneself the Eternal Shadows.*[1] To deal with demons one must be a demon. The Devil is the spirit of Evil, the fatal current of misdirected and evil wills. To enter this current is to plunge into the abyss. Moreover the Spirit of Evil only replies to rash and unhealthy curiosity. Visions are the phenomena of drunkenness or delirium. To see spirits? What a chimera! It is as though one professed to touch music and bottle thought. If the spirits of the dead have gone out from amongst us, it is because they could no longer live here. How do you suppose they are to come back?[2]

But then it will be said, what can be the use of magic? It enables men to understand better the Truth, and desire Good in a healthier and more effective manner. It helps to heal souls and comfort bodies. It does not confer the means of doing evil with impunity, but it raises man above animal lusts. It renders man inaccessible to the agonies of desire and fear. It constitutes a divinely radiating centre,

---

[1] Very right.—E. O.

[2] All this is true, in one sense, but, as E. L. well knew, it is not the whole truth.—*Trans.*

chasing away before it phantoms and darkness, for *it knows, it wills, it* CAN, and *it holds its peace.* This is the true magic, not that of the Necromancers and Enchanters, but that of the initiated and the Magi.

True magic is a scientific force placed at the service of Reason. False magic is a blind force added to the blunders and disorders of Folly.[1]

Paradox VI.—The Imagination Realises what It Invents

BEHOLD! the greatest magician in the universe! It is she who makes the memory yield its fruit, who realises beforehand the Possible, and invents even the Impossible. To her miracles cost nothing. She transports houses and mountains through the air, places whales in the sky, and stars in the sea, gives

[1] Darkness, *bad* or evil, as given in the Codex Nazaræus, are merely a gradual waning of the Pleroma or akasic light. (*Caligo ubi exstiterat etiam exstitisse decrementum et detrimentum.*) The Sorcerer uses the grosser, the *physically* more potential principles of akasa. The Pleroma of the Greek authors of Christianity is our akasa. " Air, the ether, is the Pleroma, the space held from Eternity by the ONE existence." (Onomasticon, 13.) " *To pan pleroma tōn aionōn—universum pleroma aconum.*" (Irenaeus, I, i., p. 15.) " In him dwells all the Pleroma carnally." (Engl. vers.) " For in him dwelleth all the fulness of the Godhead bodily."—(Coloss., 2, 9.) E. O.

paradise to the hashish or opium eaters, offers kingdoms to inebriates, and makes Perette dance with joy under the milk pail. Such is Imagination.

It is to the Imagination that we owe poetry and dreams; it is she who embroiders fables and symbols on the veils of the Great Mysteries. She makes up the stories for the children, and the legends for the peasants. She makes the thundering Gods and exterminating angels appear on the hills, and the White Ladies and Virgins near the founts. She makes predictions which are accommodated to facts, or reinterpreted when they are not realised. She is the nurse of Hope and the accomplice of Despair. She gilds the aureole of the Saints, and bronzes the horns of the Devil. She heals and kills, saves some and damns others, is chaste as the Virgin or impure as Messalina. She creates enthusiasm and thus enlarges, almost beyond the limits of the possible, the empire of the Will. She creates a belief in happiness and gives it, for so long as the dream lasts.

The imagination is the crystalline lens of our mind. She refracts the luminous rays of our thoughts and magnifies the images of all our perceptions. The scope of our vision is so small that to see rightly in this narrow world we must see things larger than in nature.

People, devoid of imagination, never accomplish anything great, for everything appears to them in mean proportions. The astronomer contemplates the universe and imagines the Infinite; *the believer contemplates Nature and imagines God.* In truth, the Imagination is greater than Thought. Science is overflowed by faith, and without faith science would remain uncertain.

What is Algebra but the Imagination of pure Mathematics, and what is the Kabala but the Algebra of Ideas? The imagination of Kabalists has converted Philosophy into an exact Science by connecting ideas with numbers; the Science of Analogies is wholly a Science of Imagination, and great nations are but congeries of cold enthusiasts, who powerfully imagine glory.

Collective imaginations achieve the results of the solar microscope. Heroes, especially, grow greater after their deaths, and the fictions of opinion raise upon superb pedestals the high majesties of history. Who will ever know the exact measure of Alexander the Great, or Napoleon I? Marat and Napoleon were two little men, energetic and ambitious of renown; the one desired to free the world which the other proposed to enslave; the first desired a rivulet of blood, the other made rivers of it flow, and then bequeathed to us two invasions, the reign of his nephew, and overwhelming catastrophies; the one is execrated, the other adored; for one the gallows, [1] for the other the triumphal arch and column, and both are exaggerations—the one of infamy, the other of glory.

---

[1] In the original " *les gémonies,*" that is the Roman place of execution.—The Tyburn of Rome.—*Trans.*

It is because Marat, more disinterested and more sincere at heart than Napoleon the First, was only a raging screaming Tribune, while Napoleon was a man of genius, that is to say a despot of the human imagination. It is because the poetry of nations loves better splendid crimes than mean virtues, because the mask of Marat is a grimace that would raise laughter if it did not evoke horror, whilst the medal of Napoleon is a majesty which imposes itself on the worship of the future. These are conclusive reasons.

If imagination finds one real point of support, it is the lever of Archimedes; without a real basis, it is only a stick on which fools ride.

Relying upon scientific and reasonable hypotheses, Christopher Columbus imagined America, dared to set off to discover it, and found it. *When one knows and when one wills, one ought to have the courage to dare.*

Imagination is the Creative Power. God is the Imagination of Nature. She has her dreams and her nightmares, but these do not prevent her Epos from being glorious. The architects of the Middle Ages have sketched its outline in their magnificent Cathedrals where the carved spouts, corbels and florid ornamentation serve to bring out the pure lines of the Ogives and the placidity of the Saints. These great artists had guessed the enigma of good and evil; they understood light and its shadows.

It is the Imagination which works miracles; by an act of their imagination a few peasant children cause

churches to rise from the earth, and shake entire
populations; witness the pilgrimages of Lourdes and
La Salette. By imagination Joshua arrested the
sun, and caused the walls of Jericho to fall at the
sound of his trumpets ; by the imagination bread becomes God, and the wine of the chalice is changed
into immortal blood, and we do not profess to say, as
may be well imagined, that this is *not* so ; but this is,
as we imagine it, according to the word and on the
faith of Jesus Christ.[1]

Imagination heals the sick and makes the fortune
of celebrated physicians ; it creates homœopathy from
which so many believers derive good : it makes tables
speak, and dictates to mediums, pell mell, pages of
learned matter and the grossest ignorance, prayers
and curses. It gives horns to Moses, and to the
cuckolded husbands, making the first resemble the
Devil, and the latter either furious bulls or patient
and mild mannered oxen. It amplifies wisdom,
exaggerates folly, demands too much of truth, makes
falsehood look truthful ; at the same time it is not
falsehood for the imagination ; all that it affirms is
true as poetry, and can poetry ever tell us falsehoods ? That which she invents she creates, and that
which is created exists. To imagine the truth is to
divine, to divine is to exercise the Divine power. In
Latin they call the man who divines, *divinus*, that is

---

[1] One of our author's characteristic " *grimaces*,"
which he must have thought witty, as they could
impose on no one, but which exasperate the ordinary
readers as in equally bad faith and bad taste.—*Trans.*

to say the Divine man, and the poet is styled *vates*, that is to say, prophet.

Faith has for its object only the divinations of those who imagine the Eternal Truths. Moses, imagined Jehovah, and the cloud hung over the tabernacle. Solomon imagined the universal temple, and that temple, destroyed successively by the Assyrians and the Romans, is still standing under the name of St. Peter's of Rome. Alexander imagined the unity of nations, almost realised under Augustus, and imagined again later by Peter the Great and Napoleon the First, whose antagonisms still maintain the balance of the world.

The Imagination is the eternal go-between in light *amours*. It is by the imagination as a rule that impressible and nervous women are taken. It is often sufficient for a man to be strange or even horrible in order to be loved. The Marquess of Sade, Mirabeau, Marat, were all beloved; Cartouche and Mandrin had been so before them. Women of the world had fallen in love with Lacenaire, and we are assured that in his prison Troppmann used to receive love letters. The Don Juans and Lovelaces owe most of their successes to their evil reputations; the lordly Bluebeards never lack victims, and it is especially when the daggers of the Lanciottos are raised above them to strike that the Francesca da Riminis love to taste the forbidden fruit. That which most powerfully excites the imagination, and consequently desire, is the consciousness of danger : hence the God of the Bible, wishing the woman to become a mother, forbade her under pain of the most terrible penalties to touch the fruit which would make her yield to love.[1]

It was only in fact when they knew that they were doomed to die that the man and woman bethought themselves of providing successors. Death ploughs the ground of Love, and Love sows there the seed from which is destined to develop the Harvest of Death. It is forbidden on pain of Death to enter into Life, since all who are born are condemned to die. This is what is meant by original sin, and the birth sin, of which we can only be guilty in the persons of our parents, stretching backwards from one to another until we reach the first. The sin of birth is the consequence of the sin of Love, that nature always makes a show of forbidding to mankind in order to stimulate their longing for it.

Imagination is the Pegasus of the poets, the Hippogriff of the Paladins, the eagle of Ganymede, and the dove of Anacreon; it is the car of fire of Elias and the angel which bears away the prophets, holding them by the hairs of the head. It is the cherub with burning pincers cauterising the stammer on the trembling lips of Hai, the mysterious Proteus that must be tightly squeezed in the realms of reason to compel it to assume a human shape and to tell the truth.

---

[1] This is not the occult meaning of the Legend referred to, and this E. L. of course knew. He seems constantly to fear that he may have somewhere spoken too plainly and to feel it a duty to set his readers off on a wrong scent.—*Trans.*

Just as there is a latent heat which determines the molecular polarisation of bodies, *so there is a latent light that manifests itself in us by a sort of internal phosphorescence.* It is this which illumines and colours the phantoms of our visions and our dreams, and exhibits to us in the absence of all external light such astounding photographic pictures. It is by means of this light that we read in the memory of nature, or in the general reservoir of impressions and forms, the rudimentary germs of the Future in the archives of the Past. Somnambulism is a state of immersion of the thought in this light invisible to waking eyes, and in this universal bath, wherein are reflected all presentiments and all memories, minds meet and intelligences interpenetrate each other. Thus it is that one can guess, translate, and explain the ideas of another. It is thus that the brain of one becomes for another an open book, which it can read off readily. The wonders of lucid somnambulism have no other cause, and are explained by a series of mirages and reflections. *The interior light bears the same relation to the external light that negative electricity bears to positive electricity,* and it is on this account that phantoms appear specially at night,[1] and that sorcerers require

---

[1] Only partially on this account. There are many other reasons. The terrestrial magnetic conditions differ widely during the day and the night. The physical energy is at its lowest ebb during the night, and the more vigorous the physical powers the less scope

darkness to perform their pretended miracles; it is for this reason that the spirits and the mediums cannot produce their peculiar phenomena before all kinds of persons; they require a small sympathetic circle, predisposed to the contagious influence of that interior phosphorescence which makes the one set see and feel what would be neither visible nor sensible to the others. Then one is slowly and progressively pervaded by the life of the dream [1]; the furniture moves, pens write without being touched, men rise from the earth and remain suspended in the air. Then realities run mad, and mad ideas seem real; the seers and seeresses are insensible to pain. The convulsionaries of St. Medard begged to be beaten with logs of wood or bars of iron; somnambulists find in pure water all the flavours that the magnetizer chooses to imagine. The dead appear, hands without bodies come and touch you: but let a healthy man, or one out of sympathy with the circle enter, the oracles are silent, the hands disappear, the furniture ceases to dance, everything returns to its natural order,[2] and the members of the circle are

---

for the psychical perceptions, and there are many other factors.—*Trans.*

[1] E. L. apprently knew very little of this branch of the subject. He apparently fancied that all phenomena were subjective.—*Trans.*

[2] All this of course is a hasty generalisation, founded on insufficient data. All this *may* happen, *or* it may *not*; it will depend on the relative magnetic (I use the word for lack of a better) powers

as sulky and displeased as sleepers who have been suddenly startled out of sleep.

This light of dreams, which we might call the dark or black light, exists independently of the sun and stars, as does the light of fireflies or glow-worms; it never mingles with the visible external light, but it may leave its imprints on the brain —imprints transitory in the hallucinated, durable in the insane. Nervous organisms congested with black light become ill-regulated magnets, and produce at times on inert objects attractions or pressures, the results of which seem marvellous, especially when amplified and multiplied, as they almost always are, by the obliging imagination of the spectators; for credulity ever lends itself willingly to miracles. Weak minds are naturally inclined towards the marvellous, and it is not easy to undeceive them when they insist on being deceived.

Never has a miracle been performed for the triumph of science and reason : never has one occurred in the presence of wise and educated persons. Strange phenomena reduced to their simplest expression may excite the curiosity and stimulate the investigation of

---

of the circle and the intruder, including in the circle the influences that have been attracted to it. Plenty of such intruders, utterly sceptical and thoroughly hostile to the supposed dupers and dupes, have found their presence, and even wills, wholly inadequate to check the progress of the phenomena. —*Trans.*

men of science, but can demonstrate in no way the intervention of supernatural beings.[1]

As a fact, God only is supernatural in the sense that He is the Master of Nature. All that is not God falls necessarily into the order of Nature.[2]

We must simultaneously ignore all the Laws of Nature and all the rules of exegesis, if we are to accept literally and in a natural signification the Dogmatic and Sacramental expressions of the Scriptures and the Councils. Thus the Faith teaches us that in the Sacrament of the Eucharist there is a transubstantiation. Is this transubstantiation natural? Clearly it is not; it is mysterious and sacramental. You may substitute one substance for another, but one substance does not become another ; it is always the same substance, amalgamated or modified. Chemistry decomposes and recombines bodies, but it does not turn one thing into another,

---

[1] All this, though literally true, is grossly dishonest. As a Kabalist Eliphas Levi knew all about elementals and elementaries. Of course these are *not* supernatural, as they belong to nature, so that what he says is true in the letter, but it is false in spirit, because he knew that all his readers considered such beings supernatural, and would hence understand that he denied their existence. So with miracles ; of course these are but the results of *unknown* natural laws, so that here too what he says is true to the letter but false to the spirit, as leading the reader to infer that he denied the occurrence of what *people call* miracles.—*Trans.*

[2] Fallacy and assumption, and he knew it.—E. O.

for in that case the two things would, at the same time, be and not be.

To change literally and totally water into wine, it would be necessary to annihilate water and create wine—two absurdities. For nothing can be annihilated, and wine cannot be created without grapes.[1] To evaporate the water and substitute for it wine would be a mere conjuror's trick and not a change of substances. Bread may become flesh and wine become blood, but only by the processes of assimilation and not by transubstantiation. These dogmatical expressions must, therefore, remain restricted to the domain of Dogma and Symbols. Taken scientifically and in their natural sense they are absurdities. Dogma is the formula of imaginary realities. Note well that we say realities and not fictions. The affirmations of Dogma are realities for Faith,[2] but they are imaginary, because we can only conceive them through the imagination since they elude the analysis alike of Science and Reason.

It is the Imagination solely that performs all miracles. What in fact *is* a miracle? It is an exceptional phenomenon of which the cause is unknown. Science then holds her peace and leaves Imagination to speak, who at once proceeds to invent and assert a cause out of all measure and proportion to the effect. The crowd accept this assertion as gospel and the miracle is incontestable.

---

[1] London wine merchants could tell him a different story.—*Trans.*

[2] That is *Blind* Faith.—E. O.

All educated people know that the miracles of the Bible are Oriental exaggerations.[1] Moses took advantage of the rise and fall of the sea ; Joshua found a ford in the Jordan ; he used to breach the walls of Jericho one of those explosive compounds of which the Priests possessed the secret ; and the national Poets tell us that the sea opened, the Jordan flowed backwards, and that the walls fell of their own accord. It is the same thing with the sun arrested in its course to mark a great day of Victory.

Do we not read in the Psalms of David that the mountains have leapt like rams and the hills like lambs? Must we take this literally[2] ? The same Poet adds that stones have been changed into pools and rocks into fountains. Have we here a transubstantiation ? The theologians contend that we must take literally the words of Jesus Christ when he says of the bread, " This is My Body," and of the wine, " This is My Blood," but then we must also take his words in a literal sense when he says " I am the true vine . . .

---

[1] They know nothing of the kind ; some may be so ; some are probably very fairly accurate traditions of occult phenomena, but E. L. knew apparently very little of the physics of occultism.—*Trans.*

[2] All this is pure sophistry. Of course the two things are utterly distinct; in the one case there is clearly the use of metaphor, in the others, previously referred to, there is equally clearly an assertion of fact; the latter *may* be a fiction, but it can neither be rejected nor discredited on the score that elsewhere tropes and metaphors are employed.—*Trans.*

ye are the branches." Now was Jesus Christ truly and literally a vine ? [1]

Must we believe that the knowledge of good and evil were really and truly a tree, and that the bitter fruits of this double-stemmed tree that yields life and death were peaches or apples ? The Serpent of Eden and the Ass of Balaam, did they really speak ? People will cease to ask such questions when the men who profess to teach others cease to be as stupid as savages.

Imperturbable good sense, united to a powerful Imagination, constitute what is called Genius. The man who possesses both these forces can become entirely independent, and exercise at will a real influence on the common herd. He will create for himself, if he so will, servers and friends, unless he makes his genius subservient to some secret weakness. It is possible to have dogmatic good sense, without having practical good sense. Great men are often their own dupes ; they love glory as Orpheus loved his companion ; they go to seek it everywhere, even into Hell, and turn round at the wrong time to see if Eurydice is following them. True glory is what none can take from us ; it consists in merit, and not in the applause of the multitude ; [2] it fears not the caprices of

---

[1] This of course is a fair argument against the Roman Catholic Dogma of Transubstantiation.—*Trans.*

[2] " . . . worth is the Ocean,
Fame is but the bruit that roars along the shallows."
—*Trans.*

Destiny, because it owes nothing to chance; it loves neither tumult nor noise; it is in the silence of Earth that we enjoy the peace of Heaven.[1]

Paradox VII.—The Will Accomplishes Everything, which It Does not Desire

Prince Sakyamuni, who has been called Buddha, said that all the torments of the Human Soul had their origin in either fear or desire; and he concluded by two sentences which we may thus render—

Desire then nothing, not even Justice; wait until soon or late Heaven accomplish it.

Nirvana is not annihilation; it is, in the Order of Nature, the great appeasement.

To will without fear and without desire is the secret of the Omnipotent will.

God fears nothing; he knows that evil cannot triumph, and he desires nothing; he knows that the good will accomplish itself, but he wills that truth should be, because it is true, and that justice should be done, because it is just.

Magic ought to *will* whatever the Mage *wants.*

He wants the beauty of nature, which he enjoys in its fullness, because he never abuses it. He wants the

----

[1] The conviction of the especial fitness of each to know best his own peculiar nature and powers. Power has its illusion. Let every one accomplish his mission.—E. O.

springs to come flower laden, the roses to bloom in their beauty, the children to be happy and the women beloved.'

He wants men mutually to assist each other, to encourage the young and help the old.

He wants the eternal good to triumph over the transitory evil, and he takes part patiently and peaceably in the work of Society and Nature.

He wants order, he wants reason, he wants goodness, he wants love, and for that which he wants he works with all his strength, for thus he wins immortality and happiness.

Desiring nothing, he is rich ; fearing nothing he is free; wanting only what he ought to want, he is happy.

A Poet has said of God :—

For Him, to will is to create ; to exist, is to produce.

We may say as much of the Mage—Wishing for the good is to do good, and no existence is barren.

Job, stretched upon his dunghill, accomplished a sublime work. He gave Patience to the world.

All suffering is a giving birth; poverty brings riches, sickness health, captivity deliverance, punishment expiation and pardon ; tears are the seed of joy. Death nourishes life. For him who *knows* and loves, all is hope and happiness.

Fortune, honour, and pleasures, these are what the majority of men crave, and they never dream that

---

' I beg to demur to this latter. " *Le Mage* " wants nothing of the kind—unless, indeed, he be a Frenchman.—E.O.

pleasures are the ruin alike of fortune and of honour ; that riches produce satiety and a disgust for pleasures, and that honours are too often purchased by baseness.

What deceptions too attend these ! The miser treasures up misery, the voluptuary depraves his senses and kills his heart, and the ambitious, thinking to scale the Capitol, find only the Tarpeian rock ; the miser hungers and thirsts like Tantalus, the voluptuary turns on the wheel of Ixion, the ambitious roll the rock of Sisyphus. Their life is Hell, their end Despair.

The Mage, or, if you prefer it the Sage, welcomes pleasure, accepts riches, merits bonours, but he is never the slave of any of them. He knows how to be poor, to stint himself and suffer ; he endures willingly forgetfulness, because his happiness, which is his own, expects nothing and dreads nothing from the caprices of Fortune.

He can love without being beloved ; he can create imperishable treasures and raise himself above the level of honours, the gift of Chance.[1] What he wants he possesses, for he possesses profound peace. He regrets nothing of that which must come to an end, but he remembers with joy all that has been good for him. His hope is already a certainty ; he knows that

---

[1] In the original " *aleatoires*," a word I never met with in French and can find in no dictionary, but manifestly derived from " *aleatores*," pertaining to a gamester.—*Trans.*

Good is eternal, and that *Evil is transitory.*[1] He can enjoy solitude but he does not fear the society of man ; he is a child with children, joyous with the young, staid with the aged, patient with fools, happy with the wise.

He smiles with all who smile, he mourns with all who weep. He takes his part in all festivities, sympathises in all mournings, applauds all strength of mind, is indulgent to all weaknesses ; never offending any one, he has never to pardon, for he never thinks himself offended ; he pities those who misconceive him, and awaits the opportunity of doing them good. It is by the force of kindness that he loves to revenge himself on the ungrateful. Ready, himself, to give everything, he receives with pleasure and gratitude all that may be given him. He leans with affection on all arms stretched towards him in times of difficulty, and does not mistake for virtue the fretful pride of Rousseau. He thinks that it is doing a service to others to give them an opportunity of doing good, and he never meets with a refusal either an offer or a demand.

---

[1] He knows nothing of the kind ; what he knows he tells, viz., that Good and Evil are *both* eternal, because both are fictions of the Human imagination, and Humanity, or God in Nature, is eternal.—E. O.

I venture to submit that this is liable to misconstruction. In the absolute, in the highest transcendental sense, Good and Evil may be both fictions, but relatively to, and *quoad* conditioned existences of all degrees, Good and Evil are real.—*Trans.*

Think you that a man of such a character is not greater than a king, richer than a millionaire, more happy than a Faublas or a Sardanapalus ? Happy he who shall understand this greatness, appreciate these riches, and taste this joy and these pleasures ! He will want nothing else, and all he wants he will have.

Perfection is equilibrium, and excesses of privation are as injurious as the excesses of enjoyment. Macerations have their unhealthy epicurism, and the Fakirs love to wither away in the ecstasy of their pride. The penitent executioners of their own bodies and of their souls feel the cruelty of the God, whom they think to avenge, triumphing in them. The burners of men are those who submit to cruel self-discipline. Pope Pius V was an ascetic, and the terrible St. Dominic was a penitent, pitilessly rigorous to himself. The fanatic capable of killing himself for God is capable of killing others ; the orgies of austerity harden the heart as certainly as the orgies of pleasure.

Arrived at perfect equilibrium, the man may walk or run without fear of falling. One must be some one to deserve to exist, but one is some one to do something ; we exist only to act ; we think to speak. Reason also is the Word, but the Word is not only speech, it is life and action. We are strong, to labour ; we are learned, to teach ; we are physicians, to heal the sick. We do not light a lamp to hide it under a bushel, as Christ said. The light should be placed on a candlestick ; *each one owes himself to all, as all owe themselves to each.* We must not hide

away the talent of gold ; we must carry it to the
Bank. To live is to love, and to love is to do good.
We should desire the progress of humanity, the
prosperity of our country, the honour of our family,
the welfare of all the world. He who interests
himself in no one is a dead man who should be
forgotten.

" If any man will come after me," said Christ, " let
him deny himself, and take up his cross daily, and
follow me." To renounce oneself is to come out of
egoism in order to enter into charity. *The true life
of man is not in himself but in others.* To carry
one's cross is to bear courageously the pains and
troubles of life. All Sages have had their crosses.
Jesus before he ascended Calvary had the ingratitude
of the Jews and the folly of his disciples ; Socrates
had Xanthippe, Plato had Diogenes ; philosophy has
to be learned in the Book of Job. Happy they who
weep, said the Master, but more happy, say we, those
who know how to suffer without weeping. Fénélon,
in his Dialogues of the Dead, finds Heraclitus more
human than Democritus. Rabelais does not agree
with him ; animals weep, but man alone is capable of
laughing ; laughter is therefore more human than
tears. Laughter is the consolation of man, and
Homer made it the privilege of the Gods. The
Epitaph on the Scandinavian Hero was, " He
laughed and died."

It is true that there is the good laughter and the
bad laughter, but the good is the true, the other is
only the gobble of the turkey or the grin of the ape.

94

Good men and clever men know how to laugh, but
the wicked and fools can only snigger.' Frank
laughter is a fruit of that joy which a good conscience
gives.

The tree may be judged by its fruits, says the
Gospel ; we do not gather grapes from brambles.
*Determine, to begin with, to be really good, and
all that you do* will *be good.* The Good, the
Beautiful, the True—Virtue, Honesty, Justice—are
things inseparable, out of which grows true happiness ;
for the result of all is Peace, which is the tranquillity
of the Eternal Order.

For the will, to be powerful, must be persevering
and calm. God does not waver, says the Bible, and
we can never advance by continually halting and re-
tracing our steps. When we have sown the good
seed, we must move the earth no more, but we must
yet not cease to water what we have planted. Then
the germ will be produced, and the plant will sprout
of itself. When we have placed the leaven in the
dough, we must leave it to work. The smallest effort
constantly repeated ends by conquering all obstacles.
We ought to persevere with an invincible patience.
The most powerful men are those that do not
excite themselves, and who only act to the
purpose, with moderation and judgment. It is
the economy of labour which creates and augments
wealth. Economy, however, is not to be confounded

' This is a good old Scandinavian word, and more
nearly translates the original " *ricanner* " that either
" giggle " or " sneer," the usual translations.—*Trans.*

with avarice. The wealth of the economist is living, that of the miser is dead. The economist husbands, the miser buries; the economist spends and distributes, the miser holds and sequesters; the wealth of the economist is useful to all, that of the miser is useless to others and even to himself. The one uses, the other abuses ; the one gathers, the other monopolises; the possession of the one is property, of the other is pillage and the receipt of stolen property.

Man assuredly has no right to live only for himself ; his rule of conduct cannot be his own caprice. A child of nature, he must respect its laws; a member of society, he must accept its duties. His will may make him sovereign, but it is solely on condition of his being a constitutional sovereign ; all disorderly wills are shipwrecked and go to pieces. Every caprice is a foolish expenditure of life, and a step towards death.

To will effectively, we must will correctly and justly. To will correctly, we must judge rationally of things and not allow ourselves to be carried away by prejudice or passion.

The opinion of the common herd is not the rule of conduct of the sage. He does not overtly attack it, but he does not conform to it.

There is, moreover, at the root of all popular opinions some truth misunderstood. To have power and enjoyment fascinates and attracts all men, and truly to have power and enjoy oneself constitutes the fullness of human life. In what then do the fools

differ from the sages ? In that the former take the
means for the end, and it results that the greatest
good becomes for them the greatest evil. To have
everything except intelligence and reason—what
luxury of misery ! To have all power to do evil—
what a horrible doom ! To enjoy the abuse—what
suicide ! Is a coward a warrior because he has grand
weapons ? *Is a pig a man because it eats truffles off a
golden plate* ? Can one be proud of commanding
others when one is not master of one's self ? Alexan -
der the Great conquered the Indians and the Persians
and was unable to conquer his own intemperance.
Master of the World, he yields to a fit of fury and
slays his friend Clytus. It seemed as he were about
to rend asunder a universe too narrow to contain him,
and he bursts with wine in a frantic revel ! He dies
of delirium tremens. This man, now God, now brute,
had made nations tremble before his ambitious
madness. He dies young, like all exaggerated hopes,
and the abortion of this gigantesque existence is a
fraud upon glory. What nothingness after so much
glory ! What idle renown evaporates around that
little corpse ! and was it not of him that Jesus
thought when he said, " What shall it profit a man if
he shall gain the whole world, and lose his own soul ? "

The frog in the fable swells itself out trying to
become monstrous, and ends by bursting, and even if
a man, void of Reason, did succeed in aggrandising
himself beyond measure, what could he become save
a gigantic unreason, an enormous folly, a more in-
tense shadow to be pierced with all the brighter flash

by the smallest spark of Reason ? For, whether on the thrones of science or power, or in the most humble condition, Reason is ever the same ; she is the light of God ! Reason is like the Host consecrated by Catholic belief, the Host of which the most imperceptible fragments contain or rather express God in his fullness. Where Reason is, there is divinity. What Reason wills, God wills. The reasonable being participates in the divine Royalty. He wills because Reason wills, and his will is invincible. He can say like Christ, I am the principle that speaks. He may have his opponents, his persecutors, his oppressors, but he has no masters on earth and his equals are in Heaven.

The sun which shines upon an insect is not less glorious than the sun which renders the moon resplendent, and a beggar in the right is superior to a prince who is in the wrong.

Diogenes with good reason preferred one ray of the sun to the shadow of Alexander, and the cynic proved himself the equal of the conqueror whose power he limited by his own right not to be troubled. To desire nothing, to fear nothing, and to will patiently what is just, this is to be greater and stronger than all the masters of the earth.

Synthetic Recapitulation

MAGIC AND MAGISM

THE name of magic, after having been so dreaded and so execrated in the Middle Ages, has become in our days almost ridiculous. A man who seriously occupies himself with Magic will hardly pass as a reasonable being unless set down as a physician and a quack. Credulous folks suppose that all magicians are workers of wonders, and being moreover convinced that only the Saints of their Communion have the right to perform miracles, attribute the ideas and phenomena of magic to the influence of the Devil or evil Spirits. For our part we believe that the miracles of the Saints, and those which are attributed to demons, are alike the natural results of causes which are abnormally brought into action. Nature never disturbs herself; her standing miracle is immutable and eternal order.

Moreover Magic must not be confounded with Magism. Magic is an occult force, and Magism is a doctrine which changes this force into a power . A Magician without Magism is only a Sorcerer. A magist without magic *is only one who* KNOWS. The author of this work is a magist who does not practise magic; [1] he is a man of study and not a man of phenomena. [2] He does not claim to be either a

---

[1] His incessant struggles with the " idea " rooted in him by his unhappy Catholico-Romanism, having occupied and wasted all his time.—E. O.

[2] It is at least questionable whether this be not the best, wisest, and safest position. Admitting that by a devotion to Occult Physics, two supreme gifts are attainable,—one, the preservation of the individual memory right through all the further lives on this and the other planets of our cycle, throughout a complete circuit—in other words the quasi-immortalisation of the personality ; and second, the power of controlling and directing our own future after death instead of being drawn into the vortex and being there disposed of while still in a passive state under the laws of affinities ; yet it is at any rate questionable whether even these, the highest gifts, which not one per cent of adepts even attain to, really profit a man in the long run. Most certainly to attain them, an utterly self-regarding life is needed in the case of men of our race. A sublime selfishness it may be, but none the less selfishness, is essential to the attainment of these highest gifts. It is at least open to doubt whether an active life of unselfishness and benevolence amongst our fellows is not more conducive to happiness in the long run. In a universe governed by a mathematical justice, we may be content to leave our future in the hands of the Eternal Laws and the immortalisation of a necessarily imperfect *personality* is a doubtful good. As for all other powers dependent on a manipulation of the Astral Essence, though doubtless susceptible of beneficial exercise on rare occasions, they hardly appear to me aims worthy of the Man-Divine. A

magician or a mage, and he can only shrug his
shoulders when he is taken for a sorcerer. He has
studied the Kabala and the magical doctrines of the
ancient sanctuaries; he feels that he understands
them, and he sincerely believes in and admires them ;
to him they are the noblest and the truest Science
that the world possesses, and he deeply regrets that
they are so little known. For this it is that he seeks
to make them better known, taking only the title of
Professor of the Highest Science. The Science of
Magism is contained in the books of the Kabala, in
the Symbols of Egypt and of India,[1] in the books of

---

certain theoretical knowledge of the Physics of
Occultism grows in the mind in its progress in the
Metaphysics of the " Highest Science," but in my
humble notion it is to a thorough comprehension and
grasp of these latter that our best efforts should be
directed. We should not waste time, seeking powers
or power ; we should lift no longing gaze even to the
two supreme accomplishments, but we should strive so
to purify our *natures* and permeate ourselves with an
active love for the ALL, as to ensure at the recast,
the evolution of a higher personality, and so to make
the cognisance of the infinite unity, and all that
thereby hangs a part of ourselves, as to render it a
necessary intuition of the new personality. This is
to be " *un vrai magiste qui ne pratique point la
magie,*" and to my mind this is, perhaps, the nobler,
though, doubtless, the less attractive path.—*Trans.*

[1] And above all in the Ancient Sacred Literature of
India. But E. Levi had never studied the *Bhagavad-
Gita* and other like incarnations of the spiritual life
in the flesh of the latter, or he would have been a far
truer " Magiste ".—*Trans.*

Hermes Trismegistus, in the oracles of Zoroaster, and in the writings of some great men of the Middle Ages, like Dante, Paracelsus, Trithemus, William Postel, Pomponaceus, Robert Fludd, etc. The works of Magic are divination or prescience, Thaumaturgy or the use of exceptional powers, and Theurgy or rule over visions and spirits.

One may divine or predict, either by observations and the inductions of wisdom, or by the intuitions of ecstasy or sleep, or by calculations of Science, or by the visions of enthusiasm, which is a species of intoxication. Indeed Paracelsus calls it "*ebrie-catum*" or a species of ebriety. The states which are connected with somnambulism, exaltation, hallucination, intoxication whether by alcohol or drugs, in a word with all classes of artificial or accidental insanity in which the phosphorescence of the brain is increased or over-excited, are dangerous and contrary to nature, and it is wrong to attempt to produce them, because they derange the nervous equilibrium, and lead almost infallibly to frenzy, catalepsy and madness.

Divination and prediction by mere sagacity demand a profound knowledge of the laws of Nature, a constant observation of phenomena and their correlation, the discernment of Spirits by the science of signs, the exact nature of analogies, and the calculation, be it integral or differential, of chances and probabilities. It is useful to divine and foresee, but we must not allow ourselves to divine or to mix ourselves up in predictions. A prophet interested in a matter is always a false prophet, because desire deranges sagacity; a prophet disinterested, that is to say a true prophet, always makes himself enemies, because there is always in this world more evil than good to predict; the occult sciences should always be kept hidden; the Initiate who speaks, profanes; *and he who knows not how to keep silence, knows nothing.*[1]

Noah foresaw the Deluge but took good care not to predict it. He held his tongue and built his ark. Joseph foresaw the seven years of famine and made his arrangements which secured to the king and priests all the wealth of Egypt. Jonah foretold the destruction of Nineveh, and fled in despair because his prediction was not accomplished. The early Christians predicted the burning of Rome, and Nero with some appearance of justice accused them of having set it on fire. The Sorcerers of Macbeth drove him to regicide, by telling him that he would be a king. Prophecy seems to attract evil and often

---

[1] " Keep silence all who enter here," has from time immemorial been graved above the Portals of Occultism, " *Gopaniyum prayatnena,*" " to be kept secret with the greatest care " is the refrain of all the ancient Aryan writers on Psychism. But valid as this insistence on secrecy has been in the past, it must not be forgotten that evolution never sleeps, and that the wheel is ever turning. A new and higher race is scintillating on the dim horizon, and what are the highest secrets of one race, and intolerable to its mass, become the intuitions, if not the palpable verities, of the next.—*Trans.*

provokes crime. The Jews believed that the glory of
God was involved in the eternal preservation of their
Temple; to predict the destruction of this edifice was
blasphemous. Jesus dared to do this, and the Jews,
who but the day before had spread their garments
beneath his feet and decked his path with branches
and palms, cried all with one voice, " Let him be
crucified!" But it was not for them that the Saviour
had made this prediction, but for the small circle of
his apostles and faithful followers; unfortunately it
became public and served as a pretext for the judicial
murder of the best and most divine of men.[1]

If we can predict exactly and certainly when
eclipses are to occur and comets to return, why
should we not be able to predict the periods of the
greatnesses and decadences of empires? Being
given the nature of a germ, do we not know what
kind of tree it will produce? Knowing the motor,
the impact and the obstacle, can we not determine
the duration and extent of the movement? Read the
book, entitled *Prognosticatio eximii docti Theoph-
rasti Paracelsi*, and you will be astounded at the
matters that this great man was able to foresee by
combining the calculations of Science with the
intuitions of a marvellous sagacity!

One may predict with certainty by help of the
calculations of science, and with *un*certainty by help

---

[1] This entire paragraph is sophistical and insincere
to a degree. It savours not of " the things which
are of God but of the things which are of man "; not
of occultism, but of Eliphas Leviism.—*Trans.*

of a sensitively impressionable nature, or magnetic intuition.

It is the same with miracles ; these are astounding phenomena because they are abnormal and are produced in accordance with certain natural laws as yet unknown. When electricity was still a mystery for the multitude, electrical phenomena were miracles. Magnetic phenomena astonish at the present day the adepts of spiritism, because science has not yet officially recognised and determined the forces of human magnetism, which is distinct, according to our view, from animal magnetism. It is not yet known to what extent the imagination and will of man are powers. It is evident that in certain cases nature obeys them : the sick suddenly recover health, inert objects change their position without any apparent motive force, visible and palpable forms are produced ; *the cause of all this is God for one set, the Devil for the other, and no one reflects that God is too great to condescend to conjuring tricks, and that the Devil, if he exists, as portrayed in legends, would be too intelligent and too proud to consent to be made ridiculous.*

All exclusive religions rely on miracles, and each attributes to the Devil the miracles of its opposing Faith. In this latter they are all to a certain extent right. The Devil is ignorance, the demons are false Gods. Now all false *Gods* perform miracles, the true God works only one, which is that of the eternal Order.

The miracles of the Gospel are the wondrous operations of the Divine Spirit, related in an enigmatical style, as is the custom of the ancients and of

Orientals especially. That spirit changes water into wine, *that is to say indifference into love* ; it walks on the waters, and with a word stills tempests ; it opens the eyes of the blind and the ears of the deaf ; it makes the dumb to speak, and the paralytic to walk. *It resuscitates humanity buried for four days (that is for four thousand years)* ; it shows it in its putrefaction like Lazarus, and ordains that it be released from its bonds and from its shroud. Such are the true miracles of Christ, but if they ask him for prodigies, he replies, " An evil and adulterous generation seeketh after a sign and there shall no sign be given to it, but that of the prophet Jonas." Here the Master gives us to understand that the miracles of the Bible are also allegories. Jonas issuing alive from the fish that has swallowed him is humanity which regenerates itself. Jesus gave to the Jews as incontestable miracles the holiness of his doctrine and the example of his virtues.

Jesus may certainly have healed the sick ; since Vespasian, Apollonius, Gassner, Mesmer, and the Zouave Jacob have also healed the sick ; sick people too may have been healed at Lourdes, as at the tomb of the deacon Paris ; but such cures are not miracles, they are the natural results of a certain exaltation in Faith. Jesus Christ said so himself. " Can you cure me ? " asked a certain sick person ; " If thou canst believe," said the Master, " all things are possible to him that believeth."

Faith produces certain apparent miracles, and credulity exaggerates them. When Jesus said that all

was possible to Faith, he did not mean by this to say
that the impossible could ever become the possible.

The impossible is that which is absolutely contrary
to the immutable laws of nature, and to the eternal
Reason.[1]

Every man is a magnetic focus, which attracts and
radiates. That attraction and that projection are
what ·are called in magic the inspiration and respir-
ation. The good inspire and respire good, the wicked
attract and respire evil ; the good may heal the body,
because they make the souls better, the wicked do
harm both to souls and bodies. Often the wicked
attract good to corrupt it, and the good attract evil
to change it into good. Thus it is that at times the
wicked seem to prosper, whilst the good are victims
of their own virtues ; but they grossly deceive themselves who fancy that Tiberius at Capri was happier
than Mary at the foot of the cross of her son.
What pleasure nevertheless was wanting to
Tiberius, what suffering to Mary ? And yet how happy
a mother,[2] how miserable an Emperor !

---

[1] Which leaves the question where it was, since
even the highest adept can never have such an ex-
haustive knowledge of those laws or that Reason, as
to be able to assert of anything that it is absolutely
contrary to them, or hence to predicate impossibility
of anything outside, as Arago said, of pure mathematics.—*Trans.*

[2] The wretched Isiacs wound their breasts and
imitate the grief of " the INFELICISSIMA MATER *Isis* "
(*Min. Felip. c* 21). The return of Isis with the body of

Honey changes to gall [1] in the mouths of the wicked and gall into honey in the mouths of the just. The innocent man, sacrificed, is deified by his punishment; the guilty man, triumphant, is branded and burnt by his diadem.

Let us now touch the dangerous and darkness-shrouded coasts of magic, the intercourse with the other world, the contact with the invisibles, Theurgy and the evocation of spirits.

Everything proves to us that there exist other intelligent beings than man. The Hierarchy of spirits must be infinite as that of bodies. The mysterious ladder of Jacob is the Biblical Symbol of this Hierarchy ascending and descending. God rests upon that ladder or rather he sustains it. We may say that that ladder is in him, or rather that it is He, Himself, for it is as a God, and to manifest God, that the Infinite ascends and descends.

At each rundle the Spirit which rises is equal to the one that descends, and can take his hand; but he still must needs follow him who ascends in front of him. This is a law which those who make evocations should seriously meditate.

Osiris is dated December 15th, and the search lasts seven days. (Plutarch).—E. O.

[1] In this and many other cases it is impossible to reproduce in English that antithesis of sound (miel-fiel), which, not unfrequently at some little sacrifice of sense, intensifies, so often, the epigrammatic character of our author's *dicta*.—*Trans*.

To ascend eternally is the hope of the blessed ; to descend eternally is the threat that weighs upon the reprobated.

Men invoke superior spirits, but they can only evoke inferior spirits.

Superior spirits whom men invoke attract them upwards ; inferior spirits whom men evoke draw them downwards.[1]

Invocation is prayer, evocation is sacrilege, except when it is a very dangerous devotion.

But the rash mortals who plunge into evocations have no thoughts of making the spirit whom they call ascend with them ; they want to lean on it to rise by, and must necessarily lose their balance in leaning on what is descending.

The spirit which descends is as a load to him who would raise it, and it necessarily drags down him who abandons himself to it ! To renounce the reason to follow the inspirations of a phantom, this is to plunge into the abyss of madness.

The great epoch of Theurgy was that of the fall of the ancient Gods. Maximus of Ephesus invoked them before Julian, because men had ceased to invoke them ; they had sunk below even the reason of the common people ; also to Julian they appeared thin, poor, and decrepit. Julian, fanaticised by the magic of the past, wished to take these infirm immortals on his back, as Æneas saved his father from the

---

[1] Correct.—E. O.

conflagration of Troy, and the arrogant philosopher fell under the burthen of his Gods.

We cannot see the Gods without dying. This is one of the most formidable axioms of ancient Theurgy, for the Gods are the immortals ; to see them we must pass out of our plane into theirs and enter into incorporeal life, and if this be possible without dying, it is only so in an imaginary or fictitious manner, or by an illusion resembling that of dreams. We must conclude that every apparition which we survive can only be a dream ; when a vision of the other world is real, either the seer dies, or rather is already dead when he sees it.[1] This which we

---

[1] Here he alludes to the voluntary trance condition or Samādhi induced according to the rules of occult science. Mediumistic trance is a mode of epilepsy.— E. O.

So, for that matter, I venture to submit, if words are used in their strict sense, is *Samādhi*. The real difference consists in the fact that a mediumistic trance is generally the result of an abnormal and quasi-defective organisation, undertaken or fallen into suddenly without the preparations essential to render it innocuous to the health, and without the mental preparations necessary to the retention of the free exercise of the mind and will, and is only partially, often not at all, under control, while *Samādhi* results from a long and careful series of exercises developing abnormal capacities in a normal organisation, and is preceded by a gradual training that protects the physical frame and habituates the mind and will to free exercise under

write has assuredly no sense for the learned materialists who do not believe in another life, but these are compelled, in defiance of all evidence, to deny the phenomena of magnetism and spiritism ; and cannot, therefore, be sincere—the true savants are those who believe.

The danger lies in believing without knowing ; for then one believes in the absurd, that is to say in the impossible. The old French language had a word to express rash belief ; it was the verb *cuyder*, whence is derived our word *outrecuidance*, which signifies a ridiculous and presumptuous confidence.

Theurgy is a dream pushed to the most terrifying realism in a man who believes himself awake. It is attained by weakening and exciting the brain, by fasts, meditations and watching. Asceticism is the father of nightmares and the creator of demons, the most grotesque and deformed. Paracelsus thought

---

conditions that would normally cripple or wholly stupefy them, and is wholly under control.

Add that from its nature the former cannot continue many days without producing death, while the latter can continue for months without the slightest injury, unless we reckon as an injury the grave disgust for earthly fleshly life that haunts the adept for a longer or shorter period after revival.

Both are epileptic in character, the one only semi-voluntary, the other wholly voluntary ; the one without, and the other with, the preliminary physical training necessary to enable the tissues and the mind to bear, unimpaired, subjection to the abnormal conditions.—*Trans*.

that real Larvæ [1] might be engendered by the nocturnal illusions of celibates. The ancients believed in the existence of *daimones*, a race of malicious genii who floated about in the atmosphere. St. Paul seems to admit these when he talks of the powers of the air against whom we have to fight; the Kabalists peopled the four elements, and named their inhabitants Sylphs, Undines, Gnomes and Salamanders. Young, hysterically disposed virgins in the middle ages used to see White Ladies appear near springs; in those days they called such phantoms fairies; nowadays when the same phenomena repeat themselves, people are persuaded that the Virgin has shown herself on earth, and they found churches and organise pilgrimages, which still bring in a great deal of money despite the decline of Faith. We must not insist in matters of Religion on enlightening the multitude too soon.[2] There are people who could no

---

This, though *true*, is a quibble. No doubt elementaries and elementals belong to the *Kāmaloka*, and are, therefore, not strictly speaking apparitions of the *other* world, but the public thinks and talks of all such comparatively immaterial existences as belonging to the other world, and so here again the plain sense of the passage is at variance with what the writer knew to be true.—*Trans.*

[1] This word scarcely as yet *in use* in English, though thoroughly Gallicised, is from the Latin, *Larva*, a ghost or spectre.—*Trans.*

[2] Sophistry.—E. O.

I quite agree, but if for " Religion " we substitute " Occultism " my friend E. O. apparently considers that the Sophistry disappears.—*Trans.*

longer believe in God if they ceased to believe in our Lady of Lourdes. Let us leave the consolation of the dream to those who do not yet know how to apply the remedy of reason to their ills. Illusions are better than despair; it is better to do good through a misconception than to do evil through the weakness of a rebellious reason and anæmia of the conscience.

Moses, in causing the construction of the Ark of Alliance, made a concession to the idolatry of the Jewish populace, and the golden calves of Samaria were later only counterfeits of the Keroubim of the ark; these Keroubim or Cherubim were two-headed Sphinxes; there were two Cherubim and four heads, one of a child, the other of a bull, the third of a lion and the fourth of an eagle. It was a reminiscence of the Gods of the Egyptians, Horus, Apis, Celurus, and Hermomphta; symbols of the four elements [1] and signs of the four cardinal points of the heaven; they served as emblems of the four cardinal virtues—prudence, temperance, strength and justice. These four hieroglyphic figures have remained in the Christian Symbology and they have been made the insignia of the four evangelists.

The Catholic Church has condemned the breakers of images, and yet well knew that images are but idols; the word idol in Greek signifies nothing else but an image, and the pagans no more believed that a statue of Jupiter was Jupiter, than we believe that an image

[1] And of the fourfold nature of man; the three pairs and the outer fleshy case and analogous universal quaternions.—*Trans.*

of the Virgin is the Virgin in person. *They* believed, as
we do, in a possible manifestation of the divinity
through such images; they had like ourselves statues
that wept, that rolled their eyes, and sang at sunrise;
we have, like them, our mythology, and the *Golden
Legend* might form a sequel to the *Metamorphoses* of
Ovid. Nothing destroys itself in the universal
Revelation, but everything transforms and continues
itself; *the manifestation of God produces itself in the
human genius by successive approximations and by
progressive changes. God is always the ideal of
human perfection, which grows in grandeur as man
raises himself.* God did not speak once, to hold his
peace ever after. He speaks, as he creates, always.

Torquemada and Fénélon were both Christians
and Catholics, and yet the God of Fénélon resembles
in nothing the God of Torquemada. St. Frances of
Sales and Father Garassus do not speak of God in at
all the same manner, and the Catholicism of
Monsignor Dupanloup hardly bears any likeness to
that of Louis Venillot.

The Protestants have levelled everything. They
have denied all they could not understand, and they
hardly understand what they affirm, but Revelation
does not retreat; she is not impoverished, but adds
always something to the mysterious riches of her
dogma; the Rabbis, to throw light on the obscurities
of the Bible, redouble the darkness in the Talmud,
and the Christian ages have given, as a sequel to and
commentaries on the incredible accounts of the
Gospels, the impossible Legends of the Lives of the

8

Saints. To those who deny the infallibility of the Church, we reply with the infallibility of the Pope. Always the enigma is made more complicated to prevent fools from guessing it, for all Dogma is a philosophical enigma.

TRINITY, or the three in one, signifies UNITY. INCARNATION, or God made man, that signifies HUMANITY. REDEMPTION, or all lost through one and saved by one, that indicates our mutual interdependence, the SOLIDARITY of the race.

UNITY, HUMANITY, SOLIDARITY, this will be the Trilogy of the future; pacific solution of the Revolutionary problem LIBERTY, EQUALITY, FRATERNITY.

Truly it is Social Unity alone that can guarantee the liberty of nations by creating Universal Right; it is before Humanity alone and not before Nature that men are equal; and it is the mutual interdependence or solidarity which alone proves fraternity. But how many ages must elapse before these Truths, simple as they are, will be understood?

Catholicism is official occultism and rests entirely upon mystery. The secret of the sanctuaries has been profaned, but has not been explained.

Œdipus thought to kill the Sphinx, and the plague fell upon Thebes. His hostile brothers still fight and slay each other once more. The grand Symbols of the Past are the prophecies of the Future; mysteries and miracles, such must be the Religion for the masses whom it is essential to make feel keenly what they do not understand, so that they may permit themselves to be led. This is the secret of the sanctuary, and the magists of all times have understood it. The weak can only remain united under the surveillance and responsibility of the strong ; the strong emancipate themselves. If there had never been shepherds, there would have been no tame sheep ; if dogs were free, that is to say wild, they would have to be hunted like wolves : and truly, the vulgar are either wolves or sheep ; it is servitude alone that saves them.

The great secret of Freemasonry is nothing else than the science of nature. It has long since been divulged, but people still swear to preserve it eternally, thus rendering homage to the eternal principle of occultism.

The true Initiates are shepherds and conquerors, they raise the sheep and conquer the wolves ; this was, in the beginning, the sublime mission of the Church, but in this sheepfold of the Lord, the wolves have become shepherds and the flocks have fled away.

The true Church must be one, and not divided into numerous sects ; it must be holy, and not hypocritical or greedy ; it must be universal, and not restricted to a privileged circle that repels almost the whole of Humanity. In a word it must attach itself to a common centre, which in the Roman world was Rome, but which is no more irrevocably Rome than Jerusalem. "The wind bloweth where it listeth," said the Master, and so is every one that is born of the Spirit. ". . . wheresoever the body is, thither will the eagles be gathered together."

The Catholic Church ought to be the House Mother of universal indulgence. She does not tolerate merely, she absolves; she ought to excommunicate religious hatreds and bless even her children who have strayed. It is through the Catholic faith that all sincere believers, no matter what creed they profess, belong to the soul of the Church, provided they practise natural morality and seek the truth in sincerity of heart. Let only a Pope appear who will loudly proclaim these consolatory truths, and invite all the nations of the earth to an universal Jubilee, and a new era will dawn for the Christian Religion.

Glory to God in all that is great, and peace and good will to men on Earth! It was by this cry of universal love that the genius of the Gospels, announced in old days the birth of the Saviour of the world.

The Official Church represents the Occult Church as the castes of society represent the natural Hierarchy; the Priests, the Nobility and the People represent the men of devotion, the men who are superior in intelligence and the men who are inferior.

The true priests of Humanity are the sincere philanthropists; the true kings are the men of genius; the true nobles, the men of intelligence and lofty sentiments; the common mass is the great flock of the voluntarily ignorant and poltroons. A simple soldier faithful to his flag is surely greater than a Marshal of France who betrays his country.

An honest rag-picker is more noble than a vicious prince; eminent men in all departments have risen from the people, and kings and queens have been seen dragging themselves through the mire. Every intelligent and virtuous man may deserve admission to the highest initiation ; the profane are only fools or knaves.

The initiate is a man of no party ; he desires only unity, mutual indulgence and peace. He has no opinions, for truth is not an opinion ; for him all hostilities are errors, and all curses, crimes.

Before the abuses of the Romish Church, protestation is a right and consequently a truth ; but Protestantism is a sect, and therefore a falsehood. Catholicity, that is to say Universality, is the character of true religion, it is therefore a truth, but Catholicism is a *party* and consequently a falsehood. When abuses have ceased, protestation will no longer have any reason to exist, and when Catholicity shall have been established throughout the world, there will be no more Catholicism at Rome.

In the meantime, as one cannot live respectably [1] without religion, and as it is impossible and absurd to stand alone in religion, since the very word religion signifies a thing that binds men to one another,[2] each can and ought to follow the usages and rights of the communion in which he was born.[3] All religions

---

[1] "*Convenablement*," the right word, most assuredly: *respectably.*—E. O.

[2] Rather it signifies that which binds together the soul,—or if you will the highest couple, the 6th principle, and the spirit, (or 7th principle or monad), and the absolute, of which this is a ray.—*Trans.*

[3] In other words we are by silence to consent to and add currency and vitality to what we think a false-

have a respectable side and a defective side. Let us
no more break each other's Idols, but let us lead all
men gently out of Idolatry. One must learn to
endure patiently in Catholic Churches the noise of the
ceremonial, and of the halberd of the Swiss, to weary
oneself in all gravity and respect in the Protestant
temples, to keep serious in the Synagogue and the
Mosque despite the muffled heads of the Rabbis and
the contortions of the Dervishes. All this must have
its time.

One religion passes away, but *Religion* remains;
one man dies, but humanity dies not; one woman
ceases to love or be lovable, but woman is ever worthy
of respect and love; one rose fades all too soon, but
the rose is an imperishable flower, and blooms anew
in every spring. Let us make use of Religions for
the sake of Religion, love men for the sake of
humanity, and women for the love of woman; let us
seek the rose amidst the roses, and we shall never
find deception or despair.

But because we are men, we must not insist on the
children being men. We must not beat them because

---

hood. There is a vast difference between tolerance
for and gentleness with what we believe to be the
errors of others, and the ease-loving timidity which
shrinks from showing by its own example that it *does*
believe them to be errors. E. Levi looks forward to a
reign of truth, but if men follow his advice, and for
the sake of *respectability* persistently bow to falsehood,
how is the usurper to be dethroned, how is the wrong
to be conquered, and the right to triumph?—*Trans.*

they fall, nor use them harshly because they do not understand things that are above their age. We must not rob them of their Punches and their dolls; they adore them; later they will break them; mamma will give them others, and papa will have nothing to say.

The Sacred Books of all nations in all times have been collections of fables; they are the books and pictures made for the instruction of children.

They are generally collective works resuming all the knowledge and all the highest aspirations of one people and one epoch. They are sacred as monuments should be, and worthy of respect, as is the memory of ancestors. The Divine Spirit has assuredly inspired them, but inspired them to men and not to Gods.

They reveal God, as the tree which grows reveals the seed planted in the earth, or as the rising dough reveals the hidden leaven. This double comparison is borrowed from Jesus Christ Himself.

We have said that the absurdities of Dogma are enigmatic; they are even more systematic. The great Initiates of the Ancient World never explained their symbols except *by* obscure symbols. God wills to be divined, because divination is divine, as the word itself sufficiently indicates. The riddle of the Sphinx is the trial of all Neophytes, and the three-headed dog watches always at the portals of the crypt of the mysteries. In Religion, to explain is to profane; to make more obscure is to reveal.

Science and Religion are as the day and night. If reason be the sun, faith is the moon.[1] In the absence of the Sun, the Moon is the sovereign of the heavens. Let us, however, not forget that it is from the Sun that she borrows all her rays, and that true Faith can never be absurd except in seeming.

Science, has not she too her mysteries? Escape if you can out of the labyrinth of the Infinite. Do indivisible molecules really exist? Endeavour to conceive substance without extension.[2] If on the contrary matter is infinitely divisible, one grain of dust may, in the infinity of time, by the infinite number of its parts, equal the infinity of space.[3] Absurdities on all sides! Ask Marphurius; he desires to explain that the polychronic evolution of analytical concepts, in the Relative, is equal to the isochronism

---

[1] These poetical illustrations are misleading. Science, *real* science, and religion are one; at most two faces of the Eternal Truth; allotropic forms of the same everlasting verity.—*Trans.*

[2] There *is no* such thing; it is only nothing that has no extension; the extension of what *we call* immaterial things may be beyond our cognisance, but *all* things have extension, and extension is the essence of *substance*, which both *is* and fills *space.*—*Trans.*

[3] Of course this is all a muddle; indivisible atoms do exist. You may say that the mind can divide them in conception, but if you could put the division into practice, the molecule would return into the unmanifested. Then he confuses matter, which is transitory, concrete and manifested, with substance, its eternal, abstract, unmanifested base.—*Trans.*

of the synthetical concept in the Absolute, and
he thence concludes that the synchretism of the
Abstract is analogous to the synchretism of the
Concrete.—*Cabricias arciturane!*

The mysteries of faith are borrowed for the most
part from the mysteries of science; for instance, is
not light *one*, in three rays of different colours? In
its triplicity it is blue, yellow and red, in its unity it
is white. This Trinity gives seven shades of colour;
here we have the sacred septenary.[1] Light produces

---

[1] The Septenary is sacred. not for one, but for a
thousand reasons. Take any seven coins or discs of
precisely the same size. Place one in the centre and
you will find that the remaining six, when arranged
round it as a belt, will exactly occupy the whole circumscribing space, each touching its neighbours
and the original central one. Add, with other
precisely similar discs, a similar second belt
outside the first, a third outside the second, a
fourth outside the third, and so on. Increase it,
as you may, each belt will only contain six more
pieces than the preceding one, with the one central
piece as the seventh. The belts will contain 6, 12, 18,
24, 3o pieces and so on, the numbers being terms of
an arithmetical progression of which the increment is
6. You may continue enlarging the circumference
till it covers the whole Gobi desert, but you will be
unable to add more than 6 for each belt to the
number of its predecessor. This may seem childish,
but we invite all the western mathematicians to
explain the *why* of it, and on this principle the
Universe both in its concrete and abstract manifestations is built up.

forms, it is incarnate in living beings, it dies to revive,
and buys back each morning our hemisphere from

Pythagoras speaks of the *Dodekahedron* as being
the " Divine "—for the first circle of *one and six* is
the *central circle*, the abstract, the *one* of nature *in
abscondito*, and the most Occult. It is composed of
the ONE, the central point, and of the *six*, the
" number of perfection " of the Kabalists, having
this perfection in itself, shared by no other, that by
the assemblage of its half, its third part, and its sixth
part (one, two and three) it is made perfect. Therefore it is called " the sign of the world," for in six
rounds the group of worlds attains its perfection, and
during the seventh enjoys felicity, and neither nature
nor beings labour or toil any more, but prepare in
their perfection for Nirvana. With the Christian
and Jewish Kabalists, it is the six days of creation
and their Sabbath.

And *seven* is called by Pythagoras " the vehicle of
Life," etc. Seven in short is the symbol of this Yug,
and Time.

The Sabæans worshipped the *seven* sons of Sabus.
The *seven* "spirits of God " in Revelation mean
simply the perfect man ; so with its *seven* stars,
lamps, etc. ; and the Chaldean " stages " of the *seven*
spheres and the *Birs Nimrud* with its *seven* stories,
symbolical of the concentric circles of the *seven*
spheres.

You moderns, who laugh at the ignorance of the
ancients, who *knew but of seven planets*, you have
never understood what was really meant by this
limited number ; nor have you given one thought to
the fact that men who presented Callisthenes (over
2,000 years ago) with records of celestial observations
extending back from their time 1.900 years, could not
have been ignorant of the existence of other planets.

the slavery of the night. Dupuis concluded thence
that Jesus Christ was the Sun ; a fine discovery ! It

And what (not *who*) is SABAOTH, and why should he
have been regarded as a creator ? How many
Christians are there who suspect that SABAOTH was
the Demiurgic number, *seven* with the Phœnicians,
who became later the Israelites ? (Read *Lydus de
Mens.* IV, 38, 74, 98, p. 112.) Seek for SABAOTH.
ADONAIOS in the " Sibylline Books," *Gallacus*, 278.
The *Demiurge* is *Iao* presiding over the *seven* circles
of the *seven* Ghebers, the *seven* spirits of fire, astral
light, *Fohat*, the seven Gabborim, or *kabiri*, the *seven
wandering stars*, and it is those wanderers who under
their collective name of *Kabar Ziv* (or Mighty Life
or Light) as a Central Point emanates and allows to
cluster round itself the *seven Dœmons.*

Compare—

The names of the seven
Impostor Dæmons in the
Codex Nazaræus.

1. Sol.
2. S p i r i t u s (H o l y
Spirit), Astro (Venus) or
Lebbat Amamet.
3. Nebu (Mercury).
4. Sin Luna, called also
Shuril and Siro.
5. Kiun (Kivan) Saturn.
6. Bel, Jupiter (life
supporter).
7. Nerig, M a r s—t h e
" son of man who despoils
the other sons of man ;
called also *Excoriatores* ".

The names of the *seven*
Skandhas or Principles.

7. Spirit, the reflection
of the ONE *Life*.
6. The spiritual soul
(*Female*).
5. The Animal Soul
(*Manas*).
4. The *Kama Rupa*—
the most dangerous and
treacherous of the Principles.
3. T h e L i f e-s o u l,
Linga sarira.
2. The Vital principle.
1. The Gross body or
material form—*per se* an
animal and a very feroci-
ous and wild one.

—E. O.

is as though one professed that a sphere of cardboard was positively the Universe.

As regards the little problem which E. O. invites Western Mathematicians to explain, it is simple enough. There is no mystery in it; it is a necessary consequence of the hypotheses involved in the premises. First the hypothesis involved in the description, to speak mathematically, of the figure we call a circle, the equality of all *radii*, and second the hypothesis that we are to use only equal circles. The proof is too long to insert, but it all proceeds from the known geometrical facts that where two circles touch, the line joining their centres passes through the point of contact; that where three circles touch the three lines joning their centres compose an equilateral and equiangular triangle; that the interior angles of a triangle are collectively equal to one-half of the angular extension round a point, and that each angle of an equilateral triangle is equal to one-sixth of this, and that consequently, only six such triangles, exactly this number and no more, can radiate from any point; that though the first belt may look circular, the second and succeeding ones cannot be constructed according to the terms of the problem except as hexagons, when again the properties (also the result of the hypothesis of construction) of the equilateral triangle come into play, and thus it is perfectly easy to demonstrate, that, not as a matter of mystery, but as a result following necessarily on the adopted premises, if there be *n* belts, then the *n*'th *must* contain six *n* discs or circles.

It seems useless to argue with Eastern adepts— from the time of the Gymnosophists, who taught Pythagoras, they have always, verbally at any rate, confounded things and their symbols. There is

Religion is a force which escapes from the impious and against which they break themselves. Punch will never succeed in killing the Devil, for the Devil is a caricature of God, and this caricature belongs to

nothing *sacred* in the *number* seven ; it is a *memoria technica* of hidden combinations, etc., which combinations, etc., are or may be held to be sacred, but as for the symbol 7, or the word *seven*, there is nothing *sacred* in either, the sanctity, if any, pertains to the mysteries they recall, and in no way to the symbol or word. Had our language called 6+1, *pig*, or used— as the symbol for this, then *pig* and—would have been as *sacred* as *seven* and 7.

On the other hand to those who ridicule and reject the facts of the occultists on the ground that according to them the universe is built up upon one numerical system, and that everything is in sevens or threes, it may be useful to point out that even in this little world of ours we have instances of the persistent adherence of nature to particular numbers. Thus 3 and multiples of this rule the inflorescence of all *endogens* and 4 and 5 that of all *exogens* ; and thousands of other instances can be given, so that the general rejection of occult views of the universe, on account of a symmetry in them, which is over hastily concluded to be unnatural, and, therefore, artificial and false, is not really warranted, even by our little learning. And as to 3 and 7, the latter grows necessarily out of the former, since 7 is the greatest possible number of products of three things taken, 1, 2 or 3 together.

As for the seven impostors, *dæmons*, these were also considered, by some, to represent the cycle of necessity, which, according to them, beginning with Mars, ran through Jupiter and Saturn to the earth,

those who have made it. It remains in their eyes, it
fascinates and pursues them. If all the blind could
coalesce to exterminate those who can see, could they
even then extinguish the Sun ?

---

and thence through Mercury and Venus to the sun.
But though the Tibetan Brotherhood tell us that
man does pass hence first to Mercury, they tell us
that the Planet on which we lived immediately
previous to our advent on this Earth was Mars and
their account of the worlds that make up our cycle
of necessity is quite different from that above referred
to. But though according to this latter Saturn, and
not Mars, was the Planet from which we last came,
it does not follow that the Planet *we call* Saturn was
really meant, or that the several Planets to which
occultism has attached the sings, and names of the
Planets known to the Astronomers of old, are *really*
these very Planets. On the contrary, as a rule it
may generally be concluded that when occultism says
anything, it means something else. Words, like the
names of planets, precious stones, minerals, plants,
etc., always had two meanings—one, the palpable
obvious one, which ; if accepted, leads entirely astray,
for the uninitiated ; and the other, the artificial one,
which gives the real fact for the initiated. This is
what has, and I maintain rightly so, brought more
discredit on occultism than anything else, and which
must engender disbelief in or contempt for it, in the
world at large, so long as it is persisted in. But the
adepts of all schools have always been so tied down,
by the vows and spiritual conditions (which it therefore no longer remains in a man's option to subsequently disregard) of the successive initiations, that
they can, in many matters, not speak save in this
deceptive phraseology, to' those not initiated, and

The masses are blind and foolish and must be led by the seers and the sages. But when those whose duty it is to lead the blind, become blind, when the keepers of the mad go mad themselves, there result falls and appalling disorders. This is the history of of all revolutions.

The use of brute force to repress disorder provokes inevitable and terrible reactions when that force has not the support of Justice and Truth: for then it becomes fateful[1] and balances, necessarily, action by reaction. War authorises reprisals, because in war,

---

these in their turn, as they progress, become by the immutable laws of the associations to which they belong, similarly tongue-tied and mind-bound ; and, as to many things, the only hope for the world at large lies in the gradual development of the higher races on earth, who will, untaught in these schools, work out anew their knowledge for themselves, and untied by laws and conditions, now rapidly becoming an anachronism, give freely of *all* their store to *all* men. In this direction the authors of *The Perfect Way* have made the first important step.

Of course, as to many matters, witness the facts given in the introduction, the adepts can speak more plainly, and are, nowadays, some of them, not so unwilling to speak as they have always hitherto been, but there remain the highest and most important laws of which, I am informed, they neither *will* nor *can* speak, save only to those who have been initiated, and are therefore for ever precluded from revealing the truth to any non-initiated.—*Trans.*

[1] There is no English equivalent for "*fatale*," in the sense in which it is here used, and which is not

according to the cynical saying of a great German
diplomatist, it is might that makes right ; and indeed
despotism, whether of kings or mobs, is war ; the
authority of the Law and the empire of Justice is
peace. Social Unity is the end and aim of civilisation
and transcendental politics, an end at which, from
the time of Nimrod, all great conquerors and
profound statesmen have aimed. The Assyrians, the
Medes, the Persians, the Greeks, the Romans, all
sought to absorb the world. Bacchus, Hercules,
Alexander, Cæsar, Peter the Great, Napoleon, had
no other dream ; the Popes thought to realise it
under the name of Religion, and it was a grand idea ;
but Germany nowadays opposes mathematics to the
enthusiastic onrush of beliefs, and swells day by day
her exchequer. The Emperor, one of the two pillars
of the world, is now again erect, and he is no longer
Roman. Rome on one side, and on the other the
whole world—the balance is no longer equal ; we
should necessarily require a cosmopolitan Pope,
when we had an universal Emperor.

High magic is at once Religion and Science. This
alone harmonises contraries by explaining the laws of
equilibrium and of analogies. This alone can make
sovereign Pontiffs infallible and Monarchs absolute ;
the Sacerdotal art is also the Royal art, and Count
Joseph de Maistre was not deceived when, despairing
of extinguished beliefs and enfeebled powers, he

" fatal," but that has become a thing of Fate,
operating therefore in a blind, unintelligent, irresponsi-
ble manner under blind laws.—*Trans.*

turned his glances, against his will, towards the
sanctuaries of Occultism. It is thence that salvation
will come, and already it is revealing itself to the
most advanced intelligences.

Freemasonry, which has so frightened the Court
of Rome, is not so terrible as people think; it has
lost its ancient lights, but has preserved its symbols
and its rites which belong to Occult Philosophy; it
still gives the titles and the ribbons of the Rosy
Cross, but the true Rosicrucians are no longer in its
Lodges; they are what they have been from the
beginning—philosophers and *unknown*. Paschalis,
Martines and St. Martin have successors who do not
meet in regular assemblies. Their Lodge is said to
be in the great Pyramid of Egypt, an expression,
allegorical and mystical, which the innocent and
ignorant are at liberty to take literally.

There is one thing more incontestably infallible
than the Pope, and that is mathematics. Truths
rigorously demonstrated force the mind to supposi-
tions which we may call the necessary hypotheses.
These hypotheses, if I may so express myself, are
the scientific objects of Faith. But the imagination,
exalted by an infinite want to believe and love, draws
incessantly from this rational objective paradoxical
deductions; to curb licence and mystic fantasies,
there must be an authority touching reason on the
one side and mysticism on the other; this authority,
dogmatically infallible, has no need to, and *cannot*,
be so scientifically. Science and Faith are the two
columns of the Temple; they support its portico.

If they were both on the same side, the structure must fall on the other.

It is their separation and parallelism which should eternally maintain equilibrium.[1]

The comprehension of this principle would put a stop to a misconception of too long standing and would bring peace to many souls. In truth between science and faith no real antagonism can subsist. All that has been demonstrated becomes unassailable, and it is impossible to believe in what one knows positively not to be true. Galileo knew that the earth turned, but he knew also that the authority of the Church is unassailable because the Church is necessary. The Church has no authority in matters

---

[1] Although in a certain sense this is true, it is very misleading. *Faith*, in the ordinary sense of the word, viz., a belief in that for which there is no evidence, direct or indirect, has no place in true Occultism which is an exact science, and accepts nothing which cannot either be demonstrated or at any rate proved to accord with, or follow, necessarily or with a high degree of probability, from what can be demonstrated. Of course, like all sciences, Occultism has its methods, and a man must understand these before he can understand its demonstrations; just, for instance, as a man must understand the methods of mathematical physics, before he can understand the proof that the poles of the moon describe in space a certain very complicated curve. But this latter is none the less an exactly demonstrated fact, and so too are the teachings of Occultism, although to one ignorant of the methods of this latter science they may seem absolute mysteries and matters of *Faith.—Trans.*

of science, but can oppose with all her power the
dissemination of particular scientific truths which
she judges to be at the moment prejudicial to the
Faith. People very generally believed in Galileo's
time that the popularisation of the system of Copernicus would give the lie to the Bible. Forced later
to admit that system, because it was demonstrated,
it became of course necessary to find means of recon-
ciling the difference ; the earth in fact turns, but the
Church remains infallible, even when it declares that
it is no longer itself, but our Holy Father the Pope,
who is infallible.[1]

This is not said ironically; the Pope is infallible
because it is necessary that he should be so, and he
really is so, for those who believe it, since his infallibility only extends to matters of Faith.

The work of science is to detach Faith from the
letter and attach it to the spirit; in proportion as
science rises, Faith is exalted.

The eternal Evangel is like the cloud that led the
Jews in the wilderness ; it has one face of shadow and
one face of light ; the face of shadow is its mystery,
the face of light its reason. The shadow is spread
over the letter, the light emanates from the spirit.

There is the Gospel of Faith and the Gospel of
Science. Moreover Science renders Faith impreg-
nable ; those who doubt do not know.[2]

---

[1] And thus proves again that Human Folly is
limitless as space itself.—E. O.

[2] It will be seen that by Faith *he* means the accept-
ance of the teachings of Authority (*i.e.*, of those who

Ignorant faith only preserves itself by obstinacy, and obstinacy in ignorance is only fanaticism.

Whoso believes without knowing, but without fanaticism, will very soon begin to doubt, and that doubt can only have as its result either knowledge or indifference.

We must learn, or cease to believe. To cease to believe is easier, but for the soul to cease to believe is to cease to love ; and to cease to love, is to cease to live.

Fanatics are sick, but still they are living ; the indifferent are dead.

Blind beliefs do not improve mankind ; they may restrain them through fear or allure them by hope, but fear and desire are not virtues. A dog may restrain his appetite under fear of the whip, but he none the less remains greedy, he only adds cowardice to greed. So to believe to any good purpose, we must know. It has been said that a little science detaches from God, and that a great deal of science leads us back again to Him ; this saying must be explained by stating that a commencement of Science and Philosophy detaches man *from the God of the*

---

presumably know more of the matter than ourselves) on those subjects or points on which we do not possess or are unable to obtain knowledge—a constantly varying quantity altering from moment to moment with the progress of the world and the individual, and disappearing in the sanctuary of occultism where all mysteries, at any rate of the conditioned universe, are explained.—*Trans.*

foolish, while the acquisition of much of these brings him to the *God of the wise.*

The Magist has no need to formulate his faith in God,[1] he feels in himself that supreme power of the True and the God, which animates, sustains, fortifies and consoles him. What need have we to define the light when one can see it ? What avails it to prove life, when one is alive ? When St. Paul was converted, say the Acts of the Apostles, he felt as though scales had fallen from his eyes.

The scales which cover the eyes of our souls are the vain conceits of a rash theology and the unhealthy

---

[1] And the *Mage* has not even need to *believe* in one.—E. O.

Quite so, he *has* no *need.* Occultism only deals with the conditioned universe, which *to all conditioned* in it is infinite. Admittedly, *in* that Universe only Laws, and no God, *i.e.,* no conscious, intelligent will, the source of those laws, can be traced. So the Mage may justifiably say, " I content myself with the manifested and conditioned universe and believe in no God who, whether he exists somewhere *abscondite* or not, has not seen fit to indicate himself anywhere in manifestation, and cannot therefore, (if such a being exists) *want* men to believe in Him."

But there are Mages and Mages, and there are some who say, granting all this, we yet know by a *higher* intuition that the infinite to all conditioned existence is yet not ALL, and that there is a conscious and intelligent will, the origin of those manifested laws which alone we creatures of manifestation can cognise. But this of course is a matter of Faith and pertains not to occultism proper, which is either atheistic or agnostic, but to transcendental occultism.—*Trans.*

sophisms of a false philosophy. The initiates are the seers and for the thoughtful, to see is to know, to know is to will, to will is to dare ; but to dare with success, we must *will* and know how to be silent.

" Never be zealous," said Talleyrand, and the same diplomatist averred that speech was given us to disguise our thoughts. This political mummery is not to our taste ; we do not say disguise ; we say reclothe and chastely veil that Virgin that we call thought, for *our* thought is not a thought of personal interest and falsehood ; *the Veil of the sanctuary is not like the curtain of comedy ; it is rent at times, but it never rises.*[1]

The initiate avoids with care all eccentricity; he *thinks* as do the most enlightened, and *speaks* as do the mass. If he explores cross roads it is only to reach more surely and quickly the grand route ; he knows that true thoughts are like running water. Those of the Past flow in the Present, and roll on towards the Future without our needing to toil backwards to their source to find them ; and he allows himself to be tranquilly borne onwards by the current, but he holds ever to mid-stream, never bruising himself against the rocks that line its banks.

Let us now sum up, laying down those unalterable principles that will serve alike as a basis and a crown to all we have written.

---

[1] It never *rises*, but as race follows race, and circuit succeeds to circuit, it etherialises more and more, destined to vanish wholly before the veil of the

I

Man has two means of attaining certainty—mathematics and common sense.

II

There may be truths which outrun common sense, there are none which contradict mathematics.

III

" He who, outside pure mathematics, pronounces the word *impossible,* lacks prudence," (Arago), which means that outside of pure mathematics there is no complete, universal and absolute certainty.

IV

Outside complete, universal and absolute certainty there are only beliefs or opinions.

V

Beliefs and opinions cannot be demonstrated ; men choose them as a matter of taste or accept them as a matter of policy.

VI

Useful opinions ought to be encouraged, and dangerous or noxious ones should be repressed. This explains the necessary struggle between conservatives and innovators ; *only conservatives become*

---

cosmic night, that shrouds a higher mystery and an inner sanctuary, is drawn around us.—*Trans.*

*persecutors when they consider, or affect to believe,
dangerous what is evidently useful.*[1]

VII

Pure mathematics exist by themselves; no will
produces them, no power can limit them.[2] They are

---

[1] Very feeble! who is to be the judge? What *you*
consider useful, *I* hold to be noxious, and vice versa.
—*Trans.*

[2] Our author, borrowing Pythagorean ideas, often
speaks of pure mathematics, as if they were a kind
of superhuman existence, things, as he says existing
by themselves, or self-existent. But what *are* they
really? Simply rigidly logical deductions from rigidly
limited and defined hypotheses. To say their results
are certain is merely to repeat with Oliver Wendell
Holmes, "Logic is logic, that's all I say." Given
certain accurately and exhaustively defined premises,
then logical deductions therefrom must be true.
Mathematics are the creation of the Human mind,
and depend on meanings and values and limitations
of these, which it assigns to certain symbols. There
is nothing mysterious or superhuman in them.
Change your scale of notation from the decimal to
the duodecimal, and various "eternal laws" of the
former disappear from the latter. Pass on to the
differential calculus or the calculus of Infinity in
which you introduce hypotheses not rigidly limited,
and you at once get, along with the true ones,
crowds of utterly irrelevant solutions. To say that
no will creates them and no power limits them is
absurd; they were created by the will that origi-
nated their fundamental hypotheses, and by these
are rigidly limited.—*Trans.*

eternal Laws, that no man can infringe, and from
which it is impossible to escape.

VIII

A thing may *appear* absurd and *be* true when it is
above common sense,[1] but a thing contrary to the
laws of mathematics is really and absolutely absurd,
and whoso believes in such an absurdity is a fool.

The sign of the cross, which is the intersection of
two lines, equilibrilised one by the other, has always
been considered as a divine symbol. It is the *Tau*
of the ancient Hebrews, the *Chi* (x) of the Greeks
and Christians ; in mathematics this sign+represents
the infinite, and x the unknown ; +signifies plus or
more, and the Infinite is always more.[2] Develop
science as you will, mark its first step with Alpha,
its last with Omega, and you will still always have

---

[1] Nothing is *above* common sense, but a thing may
be too ill-defined for common sense to grasp it. All
our author's sententious aphorism means, is that if
the nature, *or our knowledge*, of a thing is such that
we are unable rigorously and exhaustively to define
its premises and then argue logically from these, *look*,
to our imperfect vision, as our conclusions *may —
they may* nevertheless be true—we are in no position
to decide ; whereas, if we *can* rigorously and
exhaustively define the premises and we then argue
strictly logically from these, our conclusious must
be correct, and no one but a fool can doubt the
fact.—*Trans.*

[2] This seems quibbling. Of course the usual sign
for infinity in mathematics is ∞ —*Trans.*

before you the unknown, which you must recognise,
and your formula remains $\Omega + x$;[1] all that we
learn is wound off that unknown which is never
wholly unwound, it is this which produces all things ;
*not knowing what it is, we personify it and call
it God.*[2]

Once it *seemed* as if this personification was realised
on earth, *but the God-Man died* upon the cross, that
is on the eternal x, and the cross alone remains
for us.

X

The hypothetical personification of the Infinite can
only be infinite and excludes, necessarily, individual
unity. Every individuality is limited by some other,
unless it suppresses all others ; God, on the contrary,
being the principle of all individualities, cannot be an
individual. It is on this account that he is said to be
one in several Persons. Three is a mystic number
which represents the generation of all numbers.

XI

God never speaks to men, except through men, and
does nothing in nature save through the Laws of
Nature.

---

[1] Hence the Tibetan cross on the Dalai Lama's
headgear.—E. O.

[2] At last the cat is out of the bag.—E. O.

XII

The supernatural is that which outsteps our natural intelligence and our knowledge of the Laws of Nature.

XIII

God, even, ought not to be considered as supernatural by the Theologians, since they reason upon the Nature of God.

XIV

The Fathers at the Council of Nice have furnished a substance to God by affirming that the Son is of the same substance as the Father. Moreover if it be impossible to admit, without confounding them, a finite substance and an infinite substance, the decision of the Council of Nice might furnish arguments to the pantheists and even to the materialists.

XV

If God, as says Catholicism, has created us to know, love, and serve him, and by these means obtain eternal life, and if, as said Jesus Christ, that which we do to a neighbour we do to God, it follows that God has created men, to know, love, and serve each other and by these means attain Eternal Life.

The true worship of God, then, must be philanthropy.

And every Religion which does not inspire, augment and perfect philanthropy must be a false Religion.

XVI

A Religion, the consequence of which is the reprobation and eternal punishment of the majority of men or of some men, or even of one single man, does not inspire Philanthropy.

This does not touch the true Catholic doctrine, which only employs reprobation as a threat, and is in reality salvation offered to all men.

He who loves not remains in the death, said St. John, and those cast away by Philanthropy are those who *will* not love.

XVII

If God were, as is ridiculously supposed, an Omnipotent Personage who laid stress upon being honoured by certain special ceremonies, he would have revealed those ceremonies in a manner, evident and incontestable to all men, and there would be only one form of religious worship on earth, but such is not the case, and what he has given to all is the need and the duty of loving. Philanthropy is therefore the true and the only Religion, *really* Catholic, that is to say Universal.

XVIII

Every word of blessing and love is the Word of God, and every word of malediction and hate is the cry of Human Wickedness, which men have personified, calling it the Devil.

XIX

An act of Philanthropy, even the most imperfect, is more religious and meritorious than all the fasts, all the genuflexions, and all the prayers.

XX

The attraction which draws together the sexes is not philanthropic; on the contrary it is often the most brutal of all egoisms.

XXI

This attraction only merits the name of Love when it is sanctified by sentiments of self-devotion and sacrifice.

XXII

The man who kills a woman because she no longer loves him is a coward and an assassin, which however does not justify adultery; but all that can be said in regard to *this* has been said by Jesus Christ.

XXIII

Law should be always rigorous; Justice indulgent.

XXIV

The little suffer for the great, but the great also must answer for the little. The rich will pay the debt of the poor.[1]

---

[1] It is only in a very far-fetched or else transcendental sense that this is true. Every soul

XXV

The best things when corrupted become worse than the bad ones. What more venerable than the Priesthood, yet what more contemptible than a bad Priest? But the duties of the Priesthood are so sublime and so lifted above human nature, that every priest who is not a saint *is* bad. This explains the discredit that falls upon the Priesthood in periods when the religious sentiment is feeble. *The Gospels tell us that Christ found a good thief, but they nowhere tell us that he met with a good priest!*

XXVI

The good Priest is self-sacrifice incarnate; he is Philanthropy raised to a divine ideal; the bad Priest is one who sells prayers and takes the sacred vases for his cooking pots.

XXVII

All that *does* good *is* good; all that does ill is *bad*.

XXVIII

All that gives us pleasure *seems* to us good, and all that inconveniences or afflicts us seems bad; but we often deceive ourselves, and these errors are "the extenuating circumstances" of sin.

---

pays its *own* debts, be it or they great or small. This is the true and eternal basis alike of justice and morality.—*Trans.*

XXIX

It is impossible to love evil for its own sake, knowing what it is, and without its having some appearance of good.

XXX

Evil has no real existence, or, to put it better, it does not exist in an absolute manner. That which ought not to be, *is* not : that is certain and incontestable.[1]

---

[1] It is neither certain nor incontestable, and the whole paragraph deals in an unsatisfactory and sophistical manner with the " eternal riddle "—the origin of evil. Evil may in one sense be said to be the darkness necessary to make good apparent, but darkness is real *for us,* all the same, and so is evil.

The occultist's explanation is that evil is merely the result of the infringement of natural laws. The universe is the outcome of unaltering laws. One of these laws is evolution ; at one stage of this, sentient beings are developed, and then commences, from their ignorant transgression of the physical laws of the universe, physical evil, bodily pain and suffering. At a later stage of evolution, intelligence and moral responsibility are developed, and then, with the transgression of the moral laws of the universe by evolutes who have developed a will and moral sense of their own, moral evil commences. There is no attempt to deny the reality—*quoad* us—of evil ; *but* it is the inevitable result of the transgression of the unchanging laws of nature. It is quite admitted that the recuperative energies (the law of the reconstruction of the efficient out of the effete) of

That which we call evil exists as the shadow necessary to the manifestation of light ; metaphysical evil is error, physical evil is pain ; but error is excusable when it is involuntary. To know perfectly

nature often (perhaps always in the long run) bring good out of evil, just as the putrefying corpse is made a source of fertilisation: but the evil is as real as is, to *our* senses, the loathsome odour of putrefaction.

It is, probably, mainly the reality of evil that leads one section of occultists not merely to say " we can find no God *in* the universe," but to affirm that there *is* no God *outside* this, no intelligent conscious will as a source of the cognisable Laws. For, they argue, if there were, *he* would be responsible for all the evil, and if so he cannot be God—which means Good.

But another section argue that, conditioned as we are in the universe, we cannot draw any conclusions in regard to, or by any possibility realise or conceive, anything outside that universe, but that at the same time they have a spiritual intuition, through which, though unable to conceive Him, they *know* that there is such an intelligent conscious will, the essence of all perfection. And they add that why the adepts of the first class have no such intuition is simply because their peculiar psychical self-evolution, their psycho-physical training, renders them as incapable of spiritual intuition as the materio-physical training of ordinary athletes render these incapable of psychical intuition. The man, they say, who trains and develops what, for want of a more exact terminology, I call his psychical powers, so as to guide the laws of nature, control the elementals, and manipulate the astral light, as effectually closes the doors on his highest spiritual perceptions, as the man

that we are deceiving ourselves, and yet to persist is
no longer deceiving ourselves ; it is seeking to deceive
others. As for physical pain, it is the preservative
from, and the remedy for, the abuse of pleasure ; it
exercises the patience of the wise, admonishes the
thoughtless and chastises the wicked. It is, therefore,
rather a good than an evil.

XXXI

Disorder in nature is never more than apparent,
and all alleged miracles are either exceptional phenomena or conjuring tricks.

XXXII

When you *see* a phenomenon contrary in appearance to the laws demonstrated by Mathematics,[1] be

---

who so trains and develops his physical powers
as to win the silver sculls on the Thames, or the
champion's belt, closes the doors on his psychical as
well as his spiritual perceptions. We students can
only sit at the feet of our respective masters and
listen. We cannot form any conception of who is
right ; and one thing is certain, that, who ever be
right as to these highest transcendental mysteries,
real adepts of either class are almost as superior to
ordinary men as these are to monkeys.—*Trans.*

[1] It is difficult to understand what is meant here.
Surely the laws of mathematics demonstrate that
two do not equal and cannot take the place of one.
Yet without any *conjuring*, the occultist doubles or
reduplicates things, and that though your observation may have been perfect, and though you have
been neither duped nor hallucinated.—*Trans.*

sure either that you have observed imperfectly or
that you have been duped, or that you have been
hallucinated.

XXXIII

Truth needs no miracles, and no miracles can prove
a falsehood.

XXXIV

*The general laws of nature are known to science,
but neither all the Forces nor all the Agents are yet
known.* A glimpse has been obtained of animal
magnetism which certainly exists, but science treats
it as a problem which it has not attempted to solve.

XXXV

People always ask why the extraordinary phenomena of magnetism are never produced in the presence of men of learning.[1] It is because few men of
learning who witness a phenomenon inexplicable to
themselves would have the courage to attest its
occurrence.

XXXVI

The light that we see is only one portion of the
infinite light. It is those few rays of our sun which
are *en rapport* with our visual apparatus. Our sun

---

[1] This, though reasonable enough a score of years
ago, has now become obsolete : plenty of men of
learning have of late years witnessed and attested
them.—*Trans.*

himself is but a lamp suited to our benightedness ; it is but a point luminous in space which would be darkness to the eyes of our body, and which is resplendent for the intuition of our souls.

XXXVII

The word magnetism expresses the action and not the nature of the great universal agent which serves as mediator between thought and life. *This agent is the Infinite light or rather (for the Light is only a phenomenon) is the light bearer, the great Lucifer of Nature, the mediator between matter and spirit,*[1] *which the ignorant and impostors call the Devil,* and which is the first creature of God.

XXXVIII

What is more absurd and more impious than to give to the Devil, that is to say to Evil personified, the name of Lucifer which signifies Light-bearer ?

The intellectual Lucifer is the spirit of intelligence and love ; it is the Paraclete, it is the Holy Spirit, and the physical Lucifer is the great agent of Universal Magnetism.

XXXIX

To personify evil and make of it an intelligence, a rival to God, which can moreover understand and can no more love, this is a monstrous fiction. *To believe that God permits this evil intelligence to deceive*

---

[1] Astral Light, the storehouse of Occult Electricity ; the *vehicle* of the Primeval Chaos.—E. O.

and destroy his feeble creatures already so weak in themselves, is to make of God a personage more wicked even than the Devil; for God, in taking from the Devil the possibility of repenting and loving, himself forces him to do evil. Moreover a spirit of error and falsehood can only be a thinking folly, and does not even deserve the appellation of spirit. *The Devil is the opposite of God, therefore if God defines himself as the one who* IS, *the Devil must be he who is* NOT.

XL

We must seek the spirit of the Dogmas, while receiving in its integrity their letter, such as the sacerdotal Sphinx transmits it to us. This letter is obviously absurd, *in order* that we may seek further and higher. It is certain that to *act* one must *be*, and that to sin one must have a conscience, and that, therefore, one cannot be born guilty ; that one cannot make anything out of nothing ; that God cannot be a man, nor a man God ; that God can neither suffer nor die ; that a woman who gives birth to a child cannot be a virgin, etc., etc. No one, then, can seriously affirm the contrary of these truths, so palpable and evident, without warning us that there is a mystery in it, that is to say *a hidden sense which must be extracted and understood under pain of becoming either an unbeliever or a fool.*

XLI

That which excuses the so-called Atheists is the deplorable conception that the masses make for

themselves of God. Men have endowed Him with all
their own vices, and have imagined they were making
Him great by exaggerating these to paradoxical
proportions. Thus for an example:

Pride.—God has for object only His own Glory!
He looks for this glory in the abasement of His
rivals—as if He could have any; He tortures for
eternity His miserable creatures—for His glory;
He has killed His son—for His glory!

Avarice.—Absolute master of all good things, he
gives to the larger number of his children only
misery, and distributes his favours to the smaller
number, only slowly and parsimoniously.

Envy.—He is the jealous God. He proscribes
liberty; He leads astray the reason of the wise,
and favours by preference the ignorant and the
idiotic.

Greed.—He is never satiated with the flesh of His
victims; under the old law He required holocausts of
bulls, under the new he sniffs the steam of human
victims burning in *auto da fés*.

Luxury.—He must have Virgins like the Minotaur;
he has his seraglios of languishing amorous damsels,
and monks tortured by obscene nightmares; he
has invented celibacy to create phantoms, more
immodest than all the Roman orgies, and unnatural
dreams.

Anger.—The main topic of the sacred books and
collections of sermons is the wrath of God. His fury
lets loose pestilences, and in his implacable rage he
hollows out a hell for all eternity.

Sloth.—After a repose of an eternity, he works during six days.¹ His work consisted in giving daily one order, and after giving these six orders he felt the necessity of resting, and how was St. John wrong when, after having represented evil under the form of a monster with seven heads, he tells us that men prostrated themselves before and adored this beast?²

St. John adds that Anti-Christism must animate the image of this beast, and make it speak, and that the world will prostrate itself before this living simulacrum of human folly. *Let us beware of thinking that this could ever be realised in the person of a sovereign Pontiff of Catholicism ; doubtless reference is here made to some Antipope or perhaps to the grand Lama of Tibet !*

XLII

St. Vincent de Lerius says that that alone pertains to the true Catholic or universal Dogma, which has been admitted at all times, in all places, and by every one.³ This would simplify symbology marvellously and prodigiously enlarge the Church.

---

¹ Of course the six days represent *inter alia* the six working cycles or circuits of man—the seventh being the cycle of rest.— *Trans.*

² The correct interpretation. There was no more of a *personal* God to be found in John's ideas than in our own heads.—E. O.

³ We must go back a good deal further than St. Vincent for the " *quod semper ubique et ab omnibus.*" —*Trans.*

XLIII

It is customary to reply to those who take objections to the teachings of the Theologians, are you stronger minded than St. Augustine? Have you more genius than Bossuet? more intelligence than Fénélon? These questions are very ridiculous, when the matter at issue is one of common sense. I am certainly less versed in mathematics than Pascal, and yet had I lived in the time of that great man, and had he said or allowed it to be said before me that two and two make five, I should have reckoned his great authority as nothing, and should have continued to believe, or rather to know, that two and two make four.

XLIV

The great and learned men who have held their tongues, or have spoken in a certain manner, have had assuredly their own reasons for speaking or keeping silence. High truths are not suitable for low souls; there must be fables for children, and threats for cowards; there must be absurdities for folly and mysteries for credulity. It is through blackened glasses that we can alone gaze on the sun; looked at through a clear glass, it seems to us black, and blinds us. God is for us as a sun; we must walk by his light with lowered eyes: if one tries to gaze fixedly on Him our sight fails us. *The most dangerous and the saddest of sciences is Theology, for it constitutes itself wrongly a science of God. Rather is it a science of the foolishness of man* when it seeks to explain the inscrutable mystery of the Divine.

XLV

The light of God sparkles in us all—it is our conscience. To do the good to which this incites us and to avoid the evil against which this warns us, these are our duties towards God.

XLVI

God sows the idea in the Infinite, and the rays of the suns bring to birth the germs in the Planets. The animals have issued from the earth like the trees, but no more than the trees did they issue full formed and of full size ; species have their embryotic periods as well as the individuals of each species. To imagine that God has first moulded a statue of clay, to blow later in its face and so make of it a man, is to believe a story similar to that they tell little girls about babies being dug up out of cabbage beds. Is God denied or is Glory lessened by declining to look on him as a statuary ? It is nature that produces everything progressively and by slow degrees, operating ever through the orderly functions of the forces inherent in the substance, but it is the Divine word that guides the forces towards the ideal of the Form. Nature executes, she does not invent. The thoughts which are designed in matter come only from matter, though matter does not think. From the development of the first living cell, to the perfection of the Human Form, God has said to the forces of Nature,

" Let us make man," and his behest has endured
through many millions of years which, before him,
were but an instant. Genesis is not the natural
history of man, it is the commencement of his Religious Epopee. The Primitive couple is Human unity
established in the first family of believers. When
God diffused over the face of man a breath of
Immortality, man had already a face ; what else then
was he but one species of anthropoid animal ? Certainly man does not descend from the ape, but the
ape and man perhaps descend from the same primitive animal. Darwin's theory does not contradict
the Bible, it restores to it its character of the symbolic
Lion, exclusively religious ; the great week of the
creation is a series of Geological epochs [1] and God is
said to rest when man begins to understand that the
Universe moves on alone.[2]

XLVII

The supernatural is the eternal Paradox of the
infinite desire. Man craves to assimilate himself with
God, and he does so in the Catholic communion.
From a Rationalistic point of view and considered in
a purely natural manner, this communion is a thing
of colossal extravagance. In the Catholic Communion they eat the spirit of God and the body of a
man ! Eat a spirit, and an infinite Spirit ! What

---

[1] Or rather of cycles of development either from
zero to the monkey-man, or from the monkey-man to
Nirvana.—*Trans.*

[2] Ingenious but——*Trans.*

madness ! Eat the body of a man ! How horrible !
Theophagy, and Androphagy ! What claims to immortality ! And yet, [1] what can be more beautiful,
more soothing, more really divine than the Catholic
Communion ? The religious want, innate in man,
will never find more complete satisfaction ; and how
vividly we feel that it is true, when we believe in it.
Faith to a certain extent creates what she affirms ;
hope in the superhuman never deceives, and the
Love of the divine is never a deception.   The First

---

[1] These ever recurring " yets " and " buts " sound
odious ! He is more than humouring public superstition.   He becomes a literary flunkey in his double
dealings.—E. O.

I think my revered friend judges our author not
only harshly, in this case, but wrongly.   The shield
has two sides for the non-believer and the believer.
The cause of truth demands that both sides should be
seen and understood.   Were there not to the believer
something inexpressibly sweet and comforting in this
sacrament, would *billions* of men have derived from
it their greatest happiness in life, their chief consolation in death ? Such consolation, such happiness, may
not be for us, but it might almost be said " *Væ
victis* " for those whom TRUTH has conquered. But,
be this as it may, the very cause of Truth demands
that the court should prove its familiarity with both
sides of the case, and its verdict would carry little
weight with impartial inquirers, were this not shown.
As it is, the powerful rationalistic enunciation of the
monstrous character of the real conception, is only
brought into stronger relief by the frank admission of
the ideal beauty with which Faith is able to veil it
for believers.—*Trans.*

Communion is the coronation of the human royalty,
it is the inauguration of the serious side of life, it is
the apotheosis and the transfiguration of childhood,
it is the most pure of all joys and the most true of
all happinesses.

XLVIII

There is then something above both Nature and
Reason to explain, justify, and satisfy the highest
aspirations of both. From this point of view
the Supernatural is Natural, and the paradoxical
formula of the necessary hypotheses becomes perfectly reasonable. It is the human spirit that
constructs the Impossible in order to attain the
Infinite.

XLIX

According to the Fathers of the Church, the
Ancient Law was only an image and a shadow of the
new Law. The astonishing stories of the Bible are
but images, (they do not say allegories, the word
would have been dangerous), images of the new
dogma inaugurated by Jesus Christ, and the basis of
this dogma is that God is personally united with
humanity, and that we must love and serve God in
man ; in a word that we must love one another,
which resumes all the Law and the prophets. There
is then nothing true in the Bible which is not in con-
formity with the Gospels, and the spirit of the
Gospels is the spirit of charity.

L

To love one another and not revile, curse, excommunicate, persecute or burn each other. To love one another and consequently to assist, console, support and bless one another. Charity is Humanity endowed with a Divine Principle ; it is solidarity enriched by self-devotion ; it is the spirit of the saints, and consequently the true spirit of the Catholic or Universal Church. Those possessed with a spirit opposed to this do not belong to the Church.

But charity in the Church ought to preserve above all things the Hierarchy and unity.[1] It is rightful to protest against the abuse of authority, but not against authority itself.[2]

There exists at present a new sect of Protestants who call themselves Old Catholics, as if the child just born could call itself old, because it has had a grandfather ? But the ancestors of these ridiculous Protestants were no old Catholics, who would have

---

[1] Quite so, when the priests, as Eliphas always repeats that they *should* be, *are* all adepts of the highest occult mysteries, and the doctrines are those of the eternal wisdom religion.—*Trans.*

[2] Quite so, when authority *really* means superiority in spiritual knowledge ; but, when leaping down at a bound from this Utopian church and priesthood of his hopes, into the arena of the Catholic Church as it is, he assails the so-called Old Catholics for their schism, which after all is a step, if a small one, towards Reason and Truth, it is *he* who becomes the child and disciple of error.—*Trans.*

died a thousand times rather than separate themselves from the Hierarchy and Authority. Their
ancestors are the heretics of all ages, and their great
ancestor is Satan,¹ that unsubmitting old Catholic.

LI

If Religion is to be one, if it is to be holy, if it is
to be universal, if it is to preserve and continue the
chain of tradition, if it is to rest on a legitimate and
hierarchical authority, if it is to realise and give
what it promises, if it is to have signs of power and
consolations for all, if it is to veil for feeble visions
the eternal truths, if it is to unite in one sheaf all the
aspirations and all the hopes of the most exacting
souls, it *can* only be Catholic,² and all nations soon

---

¹ Very consistent this with what he has said above.
Is this *his* charity ?—E. O.

² Perhaps it might be said that the foregoing
neither wholly coincides with nor exhausts our
conception of the Ideal Church of the Future. But,
be this as it may, one thing is certain, viz., that on
pain of losing all vitality, it must have nothing to do
with " Catholicism," or any other name already
bristling with pre-existing conceptions and consti-
tuting a cluster of fully developed ideas, prejudices
and superstitions.

What destroyed the vitality of Christ's teachings,
turned his love and blessing into hatred and curses
for mankind, and now makes it necessary to preach
anew what he really taught ? Simply the disregard
of his warning not to put new wine into old bottles.
When the fathers of the Christian Church took in

or late will return to Catholicity when some God-
enlightened Pope boldly disavows the petty passions,
full of greed and hate, of clerical Catholicism, when
a learned clergy shall be competent to reconcile the
lights of Reason with the obscurities of Faith, and
when worship freed from material interests shall be
no longer an object of mercantile enterprise. This
will be, because it *ought* to be, and it will then be
discovered that in the Christian dogmas there are,
as in the earlier portions of the Bible, images and
shadows of the religion of the future, which already
exists and might designate itself as Messianism,
Paracletism, or better still absolute Catholicity, and
which will be the light of all spirits and the life
eternal of all souls.

---

hand to disguise and dress up the occult verities of
true Christism in the cast off and tattered garbs of
other dead or moribund faiths, they burked the new
born child as effectually as though they had buried it
with the corpses they despoiled, to furnish it with
swaddling clothes.

Theosophy may not be absolutely irreproachable
as a name for the Religion of the Future because to
scholars it is associated with doctrines and ideas
not wholly true, though having affinities with the
truth. But, to the mass of mankind the word
is a blank without associations, and scholars, unless
wilfully, are not to be thus misled. Anyhow it is
preferable to any of the names Eliphas Levi suggests,
redolent as all these are of a tyrannical and effete
dogmatism. — *Trans.*

The Great Secret

NOT to succumb to the unchangeable forces of nature, but to direct them; not to allow ourselves to be enslaved by them, but to make use of them to the benefit of immortal liberty; *this* is the great Secret of Magic.

Nature is intelligent, but she is not free. The Heavenly bodies have instinctive souls like animals, and impregnate each other; the planets are the seraglio of the sun, and the suns are the docile flock of God.

The earth has a soul which obeys the sun, under the decrees of Fate, and obeys man, instinctively.

But, for man to command the soul of the earth demands great knowledge and great wisdom, or great exaltation.[1]

Folly has its prodigies, and these more abundantly than wisdom, because wisdom does not seek prodigies, but tends naturally towards preventing their occurrence. It is said that the Devil performs miracles,

---

[1] By "*exaltation*," a word he commonly uses, he intends to signify an awakened and abnormally sensitive condition of the supersensuous faculties.— *Trans.*

and there is hardly any one but him who *does* perform them, in the sense which the ignorant masses attribute to the word. Everything that tends to estrange man from Science and Reason is assuredly the work of an evil Principle.

The sun has intelligence, but the earth is mindless ;[1] without the Sun and the labour of man she would produce nothing. The sun is her impregnator and man her accoucheur, and reluctantly and with a bad grace does she yield to the caresses of her spouse and the attendance of her physician. Animals, ill-organised ferocious beasts, noxious insects, parasitical and poisonous plants, abortions, monsters and plagues, are the fruits of her clumsiness. She resists as much as she can, and her resistance is not a crime ; she is but the creature of Law, and serves as a counterpoise to the activity of the sun. According to the hieratic tradition, man, the only son of God, ought to command the earth, but man, having infringed the law of God, has ceased to be free, and slaves are equals before slavery. The soul of the earth [2] is hostile to man, because she feels that he has no longer the right to command her ; she resists him and deceives him ; it is she who produces dreams, nightmares, visions and hallucinations, favoured in this by fanaticism,

---

[1] Truth sacrificed to literary wit.—E. O. And a great deal of the rest of the paragraph is sheer nonsense.—*Trans.*

[2] Why say earth instead of the earth's satellite ? Note that he means *moon*, whenever he mentions the soul of the earth.—E. O.

drunkenness, debauchery and all nervous disorders ; madmen, hysterical women, cataleptics and somnambulists are all under her direct influence. They call her also the astral light, and it is she who produces all the phantasmagoria of spiritualism.

We admit that the name astral light does not perfectly apply to the soul of the earth. This instinctive power of our planet manifests itself by negative electricity and magnetism ; positive electricity, heat and light come from the influence of the sun.

The soul of the earth radiates out specially during the night. The light restrains and repels its effluvia. It is at midnight, especially in the middle of the long nights of winter, that phantoms love to appear.[1]

A man is not a saint because he has visions, but one may have visions and yet be a saint, and even amongst the saints visions always involve something ridiculous or hideous. St. Teresa was tormented by blood, and believed she saw living walls, which were choking, and a Cherub armed with an arrow to lance them. Marie Alacoque saw Jesus Christ open his chest and exhibit his heart palpitating and bleeding. Martin de Gallardon saw an angel dressed as a footman ; the children of Sallette adorned the Virgin with a huge peasant's bonnet, with a yellow apron, and with roses stuck on to her feet. Bernadette Soubirons sees our Lady of Lourdes, dressed like a girl, about to take the sacrament, with a little blue

---

[1] Because there is no moon *felt* during the day as it is during the night.—E. O.

11

apron and yellow roses planted by the stalks in her naked feet. Berbignier saw Jesus Christ in the midst of several flat candlestick sockets. This vision of candle-stick sockets reappears at Pontmain, where four candles are seen fixed to the wall of the heavens and the good Virgin in the middle of them. Ravaillac saw the sacred wafers fluttering around his head and heard a voice which told him to kill Henry the IV.[1] The instinctive soul of the Earth eagerly demands blood, and favours the exaltations which lead to its shedding. Spectres, like crows, seem to scent from afar off massacres and battles. The death of Cæsar, the civil war which resulted from it and the bloody proscriptions of the Triumvirate were announced by prodigies, of which Virgil speaks. A little before the war of extermination which the Romans waged against the Jews, the Temple was crowded by visions and marvels. The morbid miracles of the convulsionaries, preceded by a short time only the hecatombs of the Revolution, followed by the great wars of the Empire : nowadays the spirits turn jugglers and the dead haunt our salons and become familiar with ladies . . . we have just passed through the war with Germany and the Commune, what have we still to expect ?

Man, the child of Earth, remains in magnetic communication with the Earth. He is himself a special magnet, which can indefinitely augment its powers by the combination of imaginations and wills. Then

---

[1] Guitean also heard a voice.—E. O.

inert objects are magnetised, and, under the influence of the physical soul of the Earth, attracted and ill-directed by man, may displace themselves, be lifted up, and cause cracking noises or raps to be heard; at times even a kind of aerial coagulation roughly models out some fugitive form : people believe they see lights or hands; dreams take to themselves bodies, and nature seems to become delirious : new pythonesses scribble at hazard new oracles, as little serious as those of the ancients : [1] the same causes produce always the same effects.

Will man ever succeed in taming entirely this whirling and devouring animal that we call the Earth? No, so long as he cannot discover a fulcrum for the lever of Archimedes, and so long as the steed is always sure of throwing its rider. In vain man torments the Earth ; the Earth will always end by swallowing him up. Hence it is that the grand dream of Prometheus, that is to say of human genius, has always been the secret of Hermes, that is to say

---

[1] The whole passage indicates either defective knowledge or possibly a desire to throw contempt on practices, of which he well knew the dangers. But the way to meet an evil thing is neither to minimise, nor misrepresent, nor pooh-pooh it, but to state it fully and fairly, and equally fully and fairly set forth its objectionable characters. This he has entirely failed to do where spiritualism is concerned. As for his sneers at ancient oracles it is scarcely honest, since he well knew that many of the ancient oracles were perfectly serious and reliable, as also why and how they were so.—*Trans.*

the discovery of a panacea for disease, old age and death,[1]

The desire for immortality, which has always exercised the human soul, is a protest against our subjection to the voracity of the Earth, but Religion has placed immortality in death, and only flatters herself that she will succeed in releasing from the slavery of Earth that portion of ourselves that she wants to raise to Heaven.

But in the language of symbolism, Heaven is spirit and Earth is matter; Heaven is light and Earth is shadow; Heaven is the good, Earth, the evil; Heaven is paradise, and Earth, hell. The Theologians moreover who believe in a local Hell can find no place

---

[1] This Panacea is not really a secret :—

Many a house of life
Hath held me—seeking ever him who wrought
These prisons of the senses, sorrow-fraught ;
    Sore was my ceaseless strife !

But now,
Thou Builder of this Tabernacle—Thou !
I know Thee ! never shalt Thou build again
    These walls of pain,
Nor raise the roof-tree of deceits, nor lay
    Fresh rafters on the clay ;
Broken Thy house is, and the ridge-pole split !
    Delusion fashioned it !
Safe pass I thence—deliverance to obtain.

The Light of Asia.

Trans.

for it save in the middle of the Earth, which seems to affirm that evil is materiality.

The Earth is lazy, because she is heavy and material, and, as laziness produces starvation, the earth engenders imperfect species reduced to devouring each other. She loves to produce beings who kill each other, because she fattens on the corpses of her children. Warfare is the inevitable condition of existence on the earth and the *raison d'être* always definitely pertains to the strongest. Might does not take precedence of Right; it constitutes it. What Darwin calls natural selection is the triumph of might.

Why are there abortions in nature? Why so many imperfect designs if the Creative Power is omnipotent? Because all Force has a Resistance as a Fulcrum, because inertia battles against movement, because shadow must equilibrise light. All is foreseen by the universal sovereign intelligence, and the Providence of God is not a direct and personal intervention.[1] If God does not create animals, he tells the earth to produce them. God has impregnated nature and nature has become a mother, producing unaided; but she husbands her efforts and simplifies her great works; she produces life, and life in its turn works on differentiating forms according to the circumscribing conditions. One effort begets other efforts, one form begets other forms, and progress is only possible through the law of transformation.

---

[1] Then it cannot properly be called Providence; who ever heard of an *im*personal intervention.—E. O.

These mysteries of nature demonstrate and explain
those of Religion which try to the utmost the Human
understanding; Divine selection, that is to say, final
salvation, coupled with the probable reprobation of
the majority; the narrow gate, regeneration or
moral transformation, the resurrection or future
transformation of the man that now is into a more
perfect being. So what has been looked on as
calculated to shatter Faith corroborates it, that
which one fancied must overthrow Religion re-
establishes it. The asserted paradoxes of Darwin
explain the oracles of Jesus Christ, and we believe
with greater assurance, because we know better what
we ought to believe. These truths will sooner or
later accomplish the conquest of opinion, and opinion
when founded on Truth always carries authority
along with it. They begin with condemning Galileo;
later they are e'en forced to admit what he asserted,
and the Church is none the less infallible, because
authority is necessary, and when she transmits her
authority to the Pope, the Pope becomes infallible
by an infallibility, authoritative, but not miraculous;
for an authority may be delegated, a miracle cannot
be delegated.

The yearning for Religion is the primary want of
the Human soul: it exists side by side with Love,
and in Love. "There exist," says Mr. Tyndall,[1] one
of the foremost scientific men of England, "there

[1] I merely translate Eliphas Levi's presentment of
what Tyndall says. I do not requote from the
original.—*Trans.*

exist other things woven into the tissue of man, such as the sentiments of veneration, respect, admiration, and not only sexual love, to which we have just referred, but the love of the Beautiful in nature, physical and moral, of poetry and art; there is also that profound sentiment that from the first dawn of History and probably for ages anterior to all History, has incorporated itself in the Religions of the world; you may laugh at these Religions, but in any case you only laugh at certain accidents of form, and you will not touch the immovable basis of the religious sentiment in the emotional nature of man. The problem of problems at this present hour is to give to this sentiment a reasonable satisfaction."

The solution of this great problem we believe that we have sufficiently plainly indicated, to enable writers better accredited than ourselves to discover it and give it with greater success to the legitimate aspirations of the world. The spirit of intelligence will come as Christ has promised us, and this will teach us all the Truth.

The doctrines of the highest science, called magic by the ancients, being no longer recognised in our days by official science, can only be presented to it under the name of Paradoxes, a word which signifies things above reason.

Paracelsus, whose name signifies an elevation of thought in some way paradoxical, designated these

the Archidoxes, that is to say, things ultra-reasonable
or more than reasonable. [1]

God is the great Archidox of the universe. Religion is Archidoxal when it appears Paradoxical.
Liberty is the Paradox or the Archidox of the
human divine.

Absolute reason, absolute knowledge, absolute
love, are Archidoxes of the human genius; imagination is Archidoxal in the creation and realisation of
its paradoxes.

The Will rushes on to the Archidox and does not
halt before Paradox.

Absolute Reason is, like the Divinity, the supreme
Archidox of the understanding; the absolute for the
mind is the unconditioned reason; the absolute for
the heart is infinite perfection; moreover, the beautiful being the refulgence of the true, infinite beauty
can only exist in the ideal personification of Truth
and Love. This personification, realised in the man,
is Christianity, realised in society as a whole it will
be Catholicity.

He who said, " I believe because it is absurd,"
gave us in a paradoxical shape the formula of the
Archidox, and, in fact alike beneath and above reason
only absurdity is to be found; but the absurdity
which lies below is nonsense and folly, while that

---

[1] This is certainly not what was intended, *Doxa*
is a doctrine or philosophic opinion; *Archi* a prefix
signifying excellence, priority, or superiority, and
by Archidoxes is meant either fundamental or
super-excellent, or highest doctrines.—*Trans.*

which floats above is enthusiasm and self-sacrifice.
Below the reason of the mass is materialism, above
the reason of the scientific is God. *Credo quia
absurdum* !

Let us now complete our Magic Paradoxes by one
last one that we will call the Gospel of Science.

Gospel of Science ! what an absurdity ! As if
Science could have a Gospel, a Bible, a Koran, a
Zend-Avesta or Vedas. All these sacred books
pertain exclusively to religion and the Priests of the
several forms of worship, and Science only concerns
herself with them, to ascertain their antiquity,
authenticity and influence on the History of nations.

There is no true Gospel but that of Jesus Christ,
but it is true that there do exist Apocryphal Gospels.

To write in the present day an Apocryphal Gospel
would be an anachronism ; to seek to give any other
dogmatic Gospel but that of Jesus Christ would be a
folly and an impiety.

We employ, therefore, the word Gospel as a
paradoxical expression, in accordance with the title
of this work which is Magical Paradoxes.

The word Gospel signifies happy news, and it
would be indeed happy news for the world to learn
that science and religion had been definitively
harmonised.

But everything comes in its due season, and the
world is not saved because an eccentric book has
been written.

Occult sciences are necessarily eccentric, for so soon
as they cease to be eccentric, they cease to be occult.

A seed is placed within the earth ; no one sees it but he who sows it, and when the earth has closed upon it, no one again sees it. Men pass close to where it is hidden, they even walk above it and for long it ferments and germinates in silence. Then a tiny shoot pierces the earth, the shoot divides into two leaves, and between these two leaves a bud appears. Thus it remains for long without any one noticing it. One day it is found that the shoot has become a sapling, then the sapling grows larger and becomes, slowly, a tree.

Then oft-times he who sowed it is himself enveloped in the earth.

He will never gather his fruits from his tree, nor sit beneath its shade.

His body fattens the earth and may cause other trees to germinate ; his thought grows in the heavens and will make other thoughts blossom. *For nothing dies ; all is transformed ; that which no longer is, shall be again, but that which was small shall be great, and that which was ill shall be better.*

This is our faith and hope—AMEN, and so be it !

---

[1] To put it more clearly : we are now well into the second half of the 4th Round, and our 5th Race (*latest sub-race of the 4th Race.—Trans.*) has discovered a *fourth* state of matter and a 4th " dimension of space ". The 5th Race has to discover, before it makes room for the 6th Race, the 5th state and dimension as the 6th and 7th Races have to find out the 6th and 7th dimensions of space and the 6th and 7th states of matter—of *their* Planet ; for the men of the 5th, 6th and 7th Rounds (or Astral circuits)

will know the states and dimensions of every thing in their solar system. Let your exact science, so proud of her achievements and discoveries, remember that the grandest hypotheses—I mean those that have now become *facts* and undeniable *truths*—have all been *guessed*, were the results of spontaneous inspiration (or intuition)—never those of scientific induction. This can scarcely be denied, since the entire history of scientific discovery is there, with hardly one or two exceptions, to prove it. Thus if Copernicus, Galileo, Kepler, Newton, Leibnitz, Crookes (even this latter as may be proved) have one and all *guessed* their grand generalisations instead of arriving at their discovery by long and painful labour, then you have in this a series of truly miraculous acts. The colossal generalisations of the ancients coupled with the paucity of their real data—generalisations that have reached us as incontrovertible axioms—are so many witnesses testifying to the untrustworthiness of our physical senses and modes of induction. The physical Law of Archimedes was not accumulated little by little—it sprang into existence suddenly—so suddenly indeed that the Philosopher who was enjoying his bath at the time, sprang out of it and rushed about the streets of Syracuse like a madman, shouting, " *Eureka, Eureka* ". When Sir H. Davy suddenly discovered Sodium by decomposing moistened potash and soda by the help of several voltaic batteries, he is said to have given vent to the most extravagant delight, jumping and hopping about his room on one leg and making faces at all who entered. Newton did not discover the law of Gravitation, that Law discovered him, dropping a visiting card as it were on his nose. Whence these *sudden* inspirations, these sudden rents of the veil of gross matter ?

Occult science not only explains but shows the infallible way of producing such visions of fact and reality. And it shows the means to reach this naturally for future generations. But the authors of *The Perfect Way* are right : woman must not be looked upon as only an appanage of man, since she was not made for his mere benefit or pleasure any more than he for hers; but the two must be realised as equal powers though unlike individualities.

Until the age of 7 the skeletons of girls do not differ in any way from those of boys, and the osteologist would be puzzled to discriminate them. Woman's mission is to become the mother of future occultists—of those who will be born without sin. On the elevation of woman the world's redemption and salvation hinge. And not till woman bursts the bonds of her sexual slavery, to which she has ever been subjected, will the world obtain an inkling of what she really is and of her proper place in the economy of nature. Old India, the India of the Rishis, made the first sounding with her plummet line in this ocean of Truth, but the post Mahabaratean India, with all her profundity of learning, has neglected and forgotten it.

The light that will come to it and to the world at large, when the latter shall discover and really appreciate the truths that underlie this vast problem of sex, will be like " the light that never shone on sea or land," and has to come to men through the Theosophical Society. That light will lead on and up to the *true spiritual intuition.* Then the world will have a race of Buddhas and Christs, for the world will have discovered that individuals *have it in their own power* to procreate Buddha-like children or—demons. When that knowledge comes, all dogmatic religions, and with these the demons, will die out.—E. O.